ORDINARY MINISTRY: EXTRAORDINARY CHALLENGE

ORDINARY MINISTRY: EXTRAORDINARY CHALLENGE

Women and the Roles of Ministry

Edited by

Norma Cook Everist

ABINGDON PRESS
Nashville

ORDINARY MINISTRY: EXTRAORDINARY CHALLENGE

This book is printed on recycled, acid-free paper.

Library of Congress Cataloging-in-Publication Data

Ordinary ministry, extraordinary challenge: women and the roles of ministry / edited by Norma Cook Everist.
    p. cm.
  ISBN 0-687-08757-0 (alk. paper)
    1. Women clergy. 2. Clergy—Office. I. Everest, Norma Cook, 1938–

  BV676 .O712 2000
  262'.14'082—dc21

                                              99-059786

Scripture quotations, unless otherwise indicated, are from the New Revised Standard Version Bible, copyright © 1989, by the Division of Christian Education of the National Council of the Churches of Christ in the United States of America.

00 01 02 03 04 05 06 07 08 09—10 9 8 7 6 5 4 3 2 1

MANUFACTURED IN THE UNITED STATES OF AMERICA

To my sister,
Marianne,
and my daughters-in-law,
Rachel and Rebecca

CONTENTS

Part One
Trusting God

Part Two
Liberating Christians

Part Three
Living Vocation

Part Four
Nurturing Community

INTRODUCTION

My son, Mark, when he was age three, said, "The lake is taking pictures of the trees." Thirty years later, while walking through the Japanese gardens in Seattle's Washington Park, I saw people reflected in the water. Then I noticed, through a play of the light, the water reflecting on the people. Theological reflection is all about light, God's light, and about people and emerging images of ministry and greater depth perception. We are called in our baptism to be ministers. We reflect on ministry and ministry reflects on us. Our ministry also reflects on the people we serve—although not in a "it-will-reflect-badly" or "well" sense. Rather, as we stop to ponder the people of God among whom we are privileged to minister, we see God at work, which in turn, calls us more deeply into our task of theological leadership.

I tried to take a picture of the reflections; however, even while focusing the camera, I realized a printed image would be inadequate. The lake was taking pictures of the people. One cannot fully capture the reflective process. The stories in this book are multidimensional, multidirectional, multifaceted reflections. And all is ordinary. This book cannot begin to capture it all, but here is a composite image anyway—a photo album of twenty-five stories, to which you, men and women, are invited to add your own. From the places where you daily walk, you are encouraged to reflect on your own images of parish leadership.

Parish Ministry

This is a book of compelling stories, images of God at work in diverse communities. The book does not present a list of "Ten Steps to . . . ," for while such books have their place, their lists of "how tos" may not fit the reader's congregation. Many people have recognized that we need new paradigms for parish ministry in this new century. In exploring such new paradigms this book includes such traditional topics as worship, education, preaching, evangelism, and administration, while it moves beyond them. It encompasses such issues indirectly, and often in their interrelationships, which is what happens in ordinary parish life in many roles. In these stories you will see how, for example, through the ministry of care one minister finds an authentic way of doing evangelism. Through the ministry of preaching, another is led to renewed educational ministry opportunities. The stories are real, and not entirely upbeat. Success stories may discourage as much as inspire. Here we trust you will find not only fresh insights, but affirmation of and encouragement for your own range of ministerial activities.

"Parish" is used in this book to include the congregation and the entire parish neighborhood, whether that be a few blocks or an entire county. The congregation includes its members, but always is poised to walk among people of other beliefs, and ready to engage those hungering for community. The congregation includes a place of gathering, but also is a place from which to go forth. You will walk with Ann around the city of San Antonio after an episode of violence. You will join in an interfaith conversation with Kim in New York. You will meet Marj responding to a call to ministry on her neighbor's farm. You will see Sister Mary Owen ministering to people "between" congregations. You will go with Mary Jo to learn from communal entrepreneurial women in Tanzania.

You are invited to think about the boundaries of your own parish. Does it encompass a particular section of town? Is it spreading beyond suburbia, until it almost meets (or doesn't meet) the country congregation? What are the patterns of people's daily interaction? Where might one find intersections of community? We need to enlarge our view of "parish" to include all the life arenas of congregation members in their ministries in daily life.

Wherever the geographic parish, people and their congregations are trying faithfully to serve contemporary society and are facing intriguing dilemmas. We live in an era of indifference to institutional religion, while at the same time pervasive, searching religious questions are posed by the daily news. We enjoy a booming "peacetime" economy yet fearfully live in a very violent culture. We can communicate instantly with the entire world, but because of the barrage of messages, we find it difficult to focus on any of them. We juggle our appointments to fit in yet one more activity, but we feel a haunting emptiness. We have learned to deal with competitive, pushing crowds, yet frequently experience intense loneliness. These are the realities of ordinary daily life.

In the midst of this time and place, our "parish," all of us, lay and ordained, are called to ministries of the good news of God's reconciling love in Jesus Christ. We want to minister effectively to individual needs. We look for the courage to help lead faith communities into a new sense of identity and purpose and mission. *Ordinary Ministry, Extraordinary Challenge* discovers the call to ministry in ordinary places among ordinary people, whose lives are complex. "Ordinary" doesn't mean "simple" or merely "unexceptional," but "usual," "normal," "customary"—the way things are supposed to be. Why would anyone want to read an "ordinary" book? In the midst of the ordinary one can find, if one can see and interpret it, extraordinary challenge. In these stories from all over the country we see Christ building the church and equipping people for their mission and ministries.

Themes

Ordinary Ministry, Extraordinary Challenge is organized around four themes: "Trusting God," "Liberating Christians," "Living Vocation" and "Nurturing Community." These titles can be read as both adjective/description and verb/action. Brief introductions to each of the four parts of the book explore these four themes. At the beginning of each chapter a paragraph invites theological reflection, focusing on the author's story, but also challenging you, as leaders in various roles, to think about your own contexts. The questions raised relate to foundational principles for parish leadership:

1. *Theology*. What theological questions arise from the stories? How does probing these questions return us again to basic tenets of the faith? What are our creedal beliefs in relation to trusting God, liberating Christians, living vocation, and nurturing community? In whom do we trust? What is the very nature of God? How does God liberate people to live Spirit-filled vocations in community? What is the nature of discipleship?

2. *Ministerial Leadership*. What insights do we gain concerning effective ministerial leadership—for leaders, and also for the entire congregation? What are the stress points of pastoral leadership today? How does one minister in the midst of apathy or conflict? From what places can one lead? How does our leadership equip people for their ministries in daily life?

3. *Contextual Realities*. What similarities and differences do we see between these stories and our own context? What is the significance of a congregation's geography, history, demographics? How might we become more thoroughly engaged in our parish reality? How do we learn from each other's situation? How does one read a context to become informed, to gain perspective, and to envision mission possibilities?

4. *Public Ministry*. What is the relationship between the personal and the corporate, the private and the public, in each story? Today the church is seen as a private, peripheral entity. Where do we see people hungering for meaning and values? How can we help people connect their daily public lives to their personal and communal faith? How do we minister in these disparate worlds? What bridges can we build?

Readers

The book presents stories suitable for private study. It also can serve as a guide for a congregation or parish board, committee, or task force. It is appropriate for clergy whose own lives are filled with ordinary and not-so-ordinary ministry. The book is appropriate for lay leaders, who in their commitment to discipleship, and ministry in daily life, wish to shape their insights into sound theological reflection. This book is appropriate for lay professionals in the church, by whatever title: diaconal ministers, deacons, deaconesses, parish associates, directors of education, youth, or outreach ministries. They will be able to identify with a particular chapter written by an author with a similar title, but also will discover insights in other chapters relating to their own ministries. The practical strategies span a broad spectrum of parish ministry so that all may see new ways to strengthen their partnerships, and bridge their personal and public ministries.

This book also is appropriate for seminary courses that connect fieldwork with theological reflection. It could be used in curricula of contextual theology, administration, parish leadership, and, in part, for courses on such specific topics as evangelism, stewardship, education, and ecumenism. *Ordinary Ministry* may even pose some intriguing questions in regard to the order *(ordo)*, the basic patterns of worship. The book seeks to present accessible help for contextual action, not through specific suggestions as to what to do when, but by provoking questions for insight and vision.

This book is written by women; it is *for* men and women readers. (One reviewer suggested we not even mention the gender, since historically authors of theological books were, without mention, all men.) Even though men traditionally have not read books written by women, or gone to see films with women in the lead roles, more and more men are beginning to say, "I find feminist theology a refreshing, productive, and liberating field," and "I've learned a great deal from women clergy in my area (or on our staff)." This book presumes we are now in an era when men, as well as women, will read and learn from resources by women authors.

Authors

The gender of authors presents an obvious, but not explicit, question: "Now that women have been ordained for a number of decades in many major Protestant denominations in the United States, do they engage in ministry differently from their male counterparts?" The answer is both, "no" and "yes."

We have come a long way in the past decades. Early books focused on the very phenomenon of women in ordained ministry. The "ordinary" signals the fact that women clergy have become no longer out of the ordinary to people who have grown up in this country since the 1970s. "Ordination," which has the same root as "ordinary," means "to be ordered." The ordained are set apart, not for special privilege, but to a specific role. Publication of this book also says that we have moved beyond "How cute," "How different," "How strange," to a time in which thousands of women are seen as providing good, solid ministry and leadership.

One helpful way to move the dialogue forward is to invite women already deeply engaged in parish ministry to write about their experiences and challenges from their own perspectives in their own voices. This book is not *about* women ministers. It is written *by* women ministers. Most of the authors are pastors; two are bishops; two are lay women; one a sister; and one a diaconal minister candidate. Women ministers were not "invented" with their entrance into ordained service. Women have been in ministry since the open tomb. To include some stories by lay authors reminds us of the importance of the ministry of all the baptized. Most of the faithful ministry of millions of women over the centuries was never recorded.

The authors write from the perspective of rural, urban, and suburban contexts, from small and large congregations. They come from the Atlantic, Pacific, and Gulf coasts, and from the heartland. Each speaks in her own voice, sometimes poetic, sometimes plain and straightforward. They represent primarily Protestant mainline Christianity, but their stories, in their ordinariness, have broad ecumenical implications.

If readers are challenged through this book to see, respect, and emulate this style of leadership, well and good. Of greater concern is that readers gain perspective for reflection on their own ministerial leadership.

Reflections on Pubic and Private Spheres

With the growing number of women entering public ministry, a significant question arises for this age and every age: the relationship between public and private spheres. Women traditionally were to remain in the private sphere of home and family. Since the nineteenth century, the church has been relegated to the private sphere in this American culture. Women in the late twentieth century challenged this society more fully by entering the public sphere previously reserved for men.

A question often raised in the 1970s to counter increasing numbers of ordained women was: If women took on clerical leadership roles in the church, would that not drive men away and ensconce the congregation even more in the private sphere? Would the church not have a lesser or a weaker voice in regard to the public issues of the day? Women entering ordained service were dubious about this fear, regarding it as one more rationale to keep them out of public ministry. Now, thirty years later, it is clear that those fears have not come true. Even though most mainline Protestant churches have faced declining membership, men did not leave the church in droves. The challenge is for men and women, lay and clergy, to discover new ways of nurturing communities for vibrant ministry in our local neighborhoods and global world.

Women never have been only in the private sphere, even though their voices were not heard authoritatively in public arenas. In researching women's religious journals published over a sixty-five-year period, I found that women addressed global and national as well as domestic issues. They were able to bridge the public and private spheres. The only challenge that remained was how they might speak authoritatively in the public world about that connection.

In visits to dozens of women leading congregations, I have seen great diversity among settings and leadership styles. But one factor characterized all the women I observed. They connect the personal and the communal, the public and the private. They do ministry differently by doing it in the ordinary relationships of daily life. Women care passionately about the outsider, about empowerment, and about liberating people with the freedom of the gospel. Women are concerned about issues in personal and family lives; they also care about the world outside the church door and about global peace and justice. What is new is that women do theology and ministry in the vernacular; the normal, daily language of the people. And they see all things in the private and public spheres as connected.

Women ministerial leaders speak the local language of the people, challenging and equipping them to reach out to connect faith with their everyday public lives in the world. Thus, to counter fears of domestication or privatization, there emerges a significant new way to be a clear witness in the world—a world so desperately looking and listening for words and actions of peacemaking and life. Herein is a vibrant paradigm for ministry, wherever we are, even in the most out-of-the-way place. Men and women are called to a ministry of liberation and life, which connects with the most personal and the most profoundly public.

Women's Place; Women's Stories

Some of the authors in this book seem to be ministering in places where it is not safe for women to be. However, one needs to remember that the places of home and family have often been the most dangerous for women. Males may have gone forth in battle to "protect" their castles, but domestic abuse killed and still kills women and children. The question is not "Is it safe for women to minister in public places?," but rather "Why are such places not safe for the people who must live there?" The issues are changing, yet sexism, racism, and classism continue, sometimes in more subtle but insidious forms.

When my husband and I lived in the inner city of Detroit, we went through the racial revolution of 1967. I was eight months' pregnant. After the riots we had much to do to help build community in the neighborhood. We had to become acquainted with and committed to each other on our block so we wouldn't kill each other. It was not safe to walk the street alone, but I went out into the public space anyway, and took my baby with me, as women through the centuries have done. Women minister in many places, and always have. No place—rural, urban, suburban—is a safe place for ministry. Women and men together are called to create global communities where we can know one another and live together without killing each other.

The women whose stories follow were invited to write about the way they do ministry. They were not assigned a topic. The convergence of images emerged. Grounded in the familiar, the stories take some surprising, even paradoxical turns. Serendipitously, an issue from one story sometimes appears in another. The women use diverse leadership styles, approaches, and are at various stages of life and ministry. A wide range of gifts in contrasting settings presented one distinctive common thread: women minister in the ordinary to open the door for the extraordinary workings of the Holy Spirit, to bring healing and new life to a divided, often violent world.

The book concludes with a biographical sketch of each author. Some include an update about their lives or ministry situation since this book was begun. The women's lives span five decades. Those ordained have been so for anywhere from four to twenty-two years.

I, as editor, offer my deepest gratitude to these women authors who said "yes," and then kept their word by doing precisely what they were invited to do—write in their own voices about real people among whom they minister. The authors become a circle of women weaving their work together, not unlike women in sewing and quilting circles through the centuries. A particular word of appreciation goes to each member of my family, each of whom serves in diverse ministries in their daily lives: to my husband, the Rev. Burton Everist, for his courageous support of women in public ministry over many decades; to our sons, Mark; Joel, and his wife, Rachel; Kirk, and his wife Rebecca, and their son Gwydion Drew. We enjoy retelling the stories of our life together.

I offer a particular word of deep appreciation to student assistants James

W. Erdman, for his extraordinary editorial collaboration; and Renee AuMiller, and Connie Rieger for their supportive, encouraging partnership. I appreciate the creative work of artists Chrysande J. Levesque and Mitzi Miyamoto. I thank faculty secretaries Patricia Schmidt and Kris Vanags Rilling for their very helpful, professional work in joining these chapters in one volume.

There are so many women's stories that are not in this book, and should be! I vividly picture Bonnie in Canada; the Anglican and Methodist deaconesses, especially Jean, in Jamaica; Karen in Australia; Rebecca and Nerita and in the Philippines; and Emma in Namibia. So many women have gone before. They ministered doing ordinary things—such as caring for a gravesite and being surprised by life, and excited to tell the good news . . . even when they were disbelieved. We can learn from reflections on the ministry of these extraordinary, ordinary women.

PART ONE
TRUSTING GOD

Belief in a trustworthy God centers human beings on a power beyond themselves. Such grounding enables one to trust and to act. "Trusting God," in both adjective and verb form, signifies that Christians believe this Creator of all the universe loves the human ones enough to entrust them with making God's image known through care for the earth and for one another. Such trust sustains when we are unable to protect ourselves; this trust must prevail when others need to be protected from our misuse and abuse of God's world.

God creates us to be steward ministers in the midst of sometimes incomprehensible pain, confusion, crisis, even catastrophe. We who claim the name of Christ dare to trust God to be not only the Righteous One, but also the Merciful One as we participate with our whole being in a ministry that trusts God is at work through us in the midst of it all.

We begin with Rebecca Ellenson, pastor in Duluth, Minnesota, where winter comes early and lasts long. She centers her story and her ministry at the altar. At that central place of sacramental ministry, she marks life's beginnings and endings with the worshiping community. But she does not stay there; she goes forth to the nursing home, to the farrowing stall, wherever God's people are all week long. Rebecca connects the ordinary patterns of worship with the ordinary patterns of daily living. How can we stand in awe in such places and learn from those among whom we minister? (A city woman in the country; or vice versa.) How can one make sense of new life and near death? How can we be priestly leaders helping people see that Christ's incarnation makes all places of ministry blessed and holy ground?

To trust in God is to listen, yes, to God, and to the ones among whom we are called to minister. Sandra Moen Kennedy is able to carefully read the context of her western Pennsylvania setting, to respect the ethnic, geographic, and familial customs of how people view death, to see how various kinds of death affect loved ones, and to understand how one grieves and remembers. Sandra allows herself to became vulnerable, but more than that, she was trusted because she trusted and respected the people. How does one open oneself to the people without inappropriately crossing boundaries? How does one minister with dignity and authenticity and also be emotionally accessible? In trusting God, Sandra became trustworthy so that people could tell their stories, and in sharing their pain enable the Spirit to heal. In her ministry of pastoral care and teaching, Sandra helps people through the healing process, leading them to claim their own gifts, as they develop skills for ministry of grief work with one another.

Listening to our own hearts may be the most difficult of all. Holly Whitcomb, a seasoned pastor, tells how she painfully became aware that her leadership was becoming dysfunctional. Her congregation colluded in codependence. Many of us confuse responsible ministry with taking the responsibility for everyone on our own shoulders. To trust God is to know we cannot be God and do not need to try to be. Where do you turn? To what holy place, holy time? Sometimes we need to leave our context. Sometimes we need to make changes in the context where we are. The Creator God created holy work and Sabbath rest. How does a minister keep rooted, grounded, trusting God in order to shape a balanced, sustainable ministry?

We need to tend the inner soul. We also need to know this God in whom we trust is a global God. Mary Jo Maass, from her small-town ministry in Mediapolis, Iowa, continues her global ministry, connecting communities in Iowa and Tanzania. How do you help people learn from one another and not learn the wrong lesson in superficial knowing? Only God is righteous, holy, judge. We, therefore, constantly are called to minister beyond our own propensity to judge. There's a wideness in God's mercy. A Tanzanian woman leads Mary Jo, who in turn leads us, to a place where women are not supposed to be. It is unsafe, not clean enough, not prim, proper, or holy. There we find women in community, not only surviving but caring for each other, women from whom the church can learn.

To trust God is to trust we will find God in surprising places, and in surprising crisis. What do you do when a tornado blows through your community? Nothing can prepare you for that day, for the devastation, for the particular challenge to ministry. Kris Ann Zierke's story leads us to ask about our own reactions in times of crisis. As the landscape is changed forever, how are we and the people changed? It is too simple to conclude, "That was a blessing in disguise." We will be called to lead at such times, and will utilize the skills we now have as well as the ones we are honing. We will need them, not only for the challenge of natural disasters, but also in the midst of apathy. Faith communities can become parochial, remaining hidden, concerned mostly with their own survival. Is the disease of apathy common in your locale? Is it contagious? We can become so involved in minutia of ministry that we literally are unprepared to deal with potential catastrophe. How do we encounter the living, all-powerful God? To trust this Creator God opens us to a range of congregational challenges we would not have imagined.

The devastation of tornado damage tests our belief in a protecting Creator; the premature death of a friend may shake our belief in the very nature of God. How can we trust the ground of one's ministry when we cannot understand what God is doing? God must have gotten this one wrong! This final chapter in Part One is really the story of two women.

Barbara Bullock-Tiffany entrusts her pastoral leadership to another when she no longer can preside, but she ministers until the end. Kathy Gerking's story includes Barbara's, who did not live to write her own. Kathy is entrusted with the ministry of being a pastoral assistant in the bishop's office, and thereby became pastor to Barbara. In our ministerial leadership we are called to a ministry of patience. God does work through process, and sometimes also through holy impatience. How do we, in the midst of our context, know the difference? In trusting God we learn God's trust in using our clarity and wisdom.

CHAPTER ONE

Ordinary Elements: Sacramental Ministry

Rebecca A. Ellenson

While handling holy things at the altar, Rebecca leads people in public worship. Follow her from that vortex into the lives of ordinary people living ordinary lives. How do we minister all week long, connecting the private and the public, the personal and the communal? How do we dare to enter holy places, handle holy things, and touch the lives of holy people with grace and awe and Word?

It was a snowy Thanksgiving weekend in Duluth, Minnesota, when I became acutely aware of myself as a mediator of the Holy. I was truly aware of my role as priest and knew I functioned as the channel I had prayed so often to become, "Lord make me an instrument of your peace. . . ." On that Friday morning, a family was gathered together because of the holiday. The grandmother's rapidly failing health lent a sense of urgency. On that gray and icy day, with the previous day's cornucopia display still on the chancel steps, we stood just inside the altar rail around the baptismal font to bathe a child's tiny head, melted snow puddling under our booted feet. The water flowed through my fingers, an ordinary element together with the holy words to claim the child for Christ. As she lay, safe in her grandmother's leukemia-weakened arms I spoke the words, "child of God, you have been sealed by the Holy Spirit and marked with the cross of Christ, forever."

The next day I found myself standing on the very same spot, the font now rolled to the side. I stood there beside a coffin because a forty-five-year-old man's heart had stopped. In the sermon just finished, I had woven the strands of his life story together with the story of God's unending grace, and drawn together memories shared by family and friends over the past few days. That time it was sand that flowed through my fingers as I sprinkled the sign of the cross onto the polished wood of the coffin and spoke the words "earth to earth, ashes to ashes, dust to dust. . . ."

When Sunday came it was time for Holy Communion and I stood again in the very same place, just inside the altar rail, robed in white, with silver plate in hand. As streams of people came forward and knelt there, I passed tiny circles of bread, one by one, flesh for flesh, from hand to hand, and spoke the words, "the body of Christ, given for you. . . ."

Ordinary Elements of Extraordinary Grace

I felt as if I were in a vortex, handling the Holy on that one spot, dispensing ordinary elements of extraordinary grace. I had seen people coming to the sanctuary all through the weekend, seeking God's grace through elements as plain as water, bread, and wine. They came bringing their common everyday reality to the sacred space, just up to or just inside the rail and I knew that no barrier could separate or contain God's grace. Our lives swirl together with God's own presence and love, filling all creation.

It was a lesson I had begun to learn one hot June day years before. I had entered the outdoor courtyard of a nursing home in a small town in southern Minnesota and saw the ninety-five-year-old woman I had come to visit. The sunlight reflected off the chrome wheels of her chair as she sat soaking in the warm rays on her skin. She asked my help in removing her other shoe so all her toes could feel the heat. After I knelt at her feet we sat together and gloried in the moment. She told me she didn't like the belt they used to keep her from falling from her chair. She didn't think it was necessary. "I'll keep trying to get them to take it off. But if I can't, well, I'll bear it," she said. "This is the life we have. We have to live it."

We went back to listening to the birds until the sun got too warm and I moved her to a shady spot under a mountain ash tree. "Oh, that's better," her gentle voice said. Then, "What's this?" as petals dropped onto her lap.

> *"Where is the home of God?" I mused.*

She breathed deeply. "Oh, my . . ." is all she said, with a look of contentment. She began to speak of the veins in her bony arms that bulged so prominently under her paper-thin skin. I had come to bring her Holy Communion, blood for blood. As I prepared the little kit with silver plate and glass cup, I considered the blood of life that still coursed so strongly through her veins and I knew that she had been priest to me that day. I was not really bringing the Holy to her, she lived in holy space already, aware of God's grace and beauty present through simple elements of nature and peaceful, quiet sharing.

The Home of God Incarnate

Another day, another year, in another nursing home beside an aged man's bed, my eight-year-old pointed me to the Holy. He stood desperate by the doorway. "Mom, I can't stay in here. Let's go. Now!" he pleaded. Quietly I told him, "Dear, I have to stay another minute or two. You can wait there by the door, or down the hall." He insisted, "No! I can't stay. Look at his nose and ears," he whispered loudly. "They're full of hair. And it smells here. We've got to go!" In his revulsion of age lay recognition of humanity shared and feared. He was wondering if his own ears would grow long and floppy too, if his own downy hair would grow coarse and wild like the eighty-nine-year-old's hair. I excused myself from the room and took my child to the aviary down the hall, listening carefully to his panic. As my child in fury and in fear allowed the bright and tiny birds to distract his mind, I returned to the room and offered an incarnate one a bit of bread and wine.

"Where is the home of God?" I mused. The words of scripture echoed in my mind, "See, the home of God is among mortals. [God] will dwell with them" (Revelation 21:3). Young and old, God is with us, Emmanuel. "What makes space holy?" I questioned. It is more than the bread and wine, more even than the words of Christ that hallow the space inside the altar rail, that hallow whatever place such elements are shared. It is Christ's own incarnation that hallows all creation. "The Word became flesh and lived among us, and we have seen his glory, . . . full of grace and truth" (John 1:14).

I remember the crisp winter day I stood next to the steel rail of a farrowing stall. A farmer in the congregation had called to invite my young child and me to watch the birth of piglets, since we were city folk relatively new to the country. Standing alongside the gigantic mother pig, many times as big as my young child, I began to realize that this visit was not about the birth of piglets or my raptly attentive child. An awareness of human frailty was palpable in the small tight-knit farming community. Over the previous weekend a neighbor had been admitted on a seventy-two-hour hold to a regional hospital's stress unit. As farmers will, they gathered by the dozen to divide the man's chores and complete long-neglected tasks. "I should have been there for him earlier," this farmer said softly as we watched the tiny pigs nuzzle and suckle.

"It took us all by surprise," I answered. We were both remembering a day, months past, when he and I and his wife sat at their kitchen table making phone calls to the same stress unit, arranging for treatment for her.

"She's doing really well now," he almost whispered.

"I know," I nodded and squeezed his arm, relief and gratitude on both our faces.

It was there, in the ripe carnal world, steam rising from the straw—in his world—where that farmer could speak of the holy matters he couldn't utter inside the hallowed walls of church. As I stood in muddy boots I heard the ring of Luke's words, "And she gave birth to her firstborn son and wrapped him in bands of cloth, and laid him in a manger, because there was no room for them in the inn" (Luke 2:7).

Christ, the Incarnate One, showed us that no matter where we are, we are standing on holy ground. As Athanasius wrote in his essay, *On the Incarnation of the Word*, in the fourth century, "No part of Creation is left void of Him. He has filled all things everywhere." In Christ, God broke down the barriers between the secular and the sacred. My priestly work flows from inside the altar rail out into the muddy world and back again.

CHAPTER TWO

Ordinary Listening: The Ministry of Grief Work

Sandra Moen Kennedy

There are certain matters that one keeps private. But when privacy turns to secrecy, the pain of not knowing takes on a power of its own. In Christ's public, undignified death, all secrets, all shame are now transformed. How does one minister so that people with grief so deep can begin to speak themselves into a new place of healing and freedom?

There are so many untold stories within any parish. Sometimes those stories are held close, like secrets. Perhaps they are experiences of mistakes made, of hopes vanished, or dreams destroyed. Very often, the untold stories are filled with loss and grief still unresolved.

As I traveled home from a hospital visit with Jean and her sister, Kay, I asked, "What was it like growing up in this small Pennsylvania mining town?" It wasn't necessary to ask much more. The stories began to flow. And as they told me about being young daughters of hard-working, stoic parents, growing up without many luxuries, they spoke clearly about the abuse their mother had endured at the hands of their father for so many years. They felt powerless to say or do anything in order to change the situation, but they resolved that they would never allow themselves, or each other, to live like that in their adult lives. And they haven't. Supporting each other as sisters and friends, each has empowered the other to meet life's difficulties head-on with fortitude and faith.

Over the years I have been impressed and inspired by the sisterhood and the commitment Jean and Kay share. Each is unique in her own way.

They give each other freedom to be an individual. But like biblical women, such as Naomi and Ruth or Mary and Martha, there is a spiritual bond between them. Even in the face of further struggle and grief, they have given each other companionship and understanding. The untold story they share, and are compelled not to repeat, has helped them to be compassionate and strong.

Sometimes the untold stories divide. The facts and feelings, the private moments of relationships, and the interpretation of events remain hidden because families are divided. The cause of pain and the effects it has played in the lives of the next generations are the tensions and inhibitors of healthy grieving.

Ellen, a woman who had separated herself from the life of a caring church, cared for her elderly mother through the months of dying from cancer. As she grieved this anticipated loss, Ellen shared her anger and sorrow about the abuse her mother experienced in a second marriage late in life. What troubled the grieving daughter most was the unwillingness of the rest of the family to admit it. Ellen knew she could not change the past, but she wanted the denial to end as a way to honor her mother's life. For the rest of Ellen's family, the untold story served to protect a respected and loved churchgoing patriarch. But for Ellen, the untold story was the continuation of pain and grief. The whole story would never be fully known; the truth that remained hidden could not set her free. Ellen found only a little relief, but sharing one piece of her sorrow was a step toward understanding and healing.

For many people, it is a new and even frightening experience to share with another person, especially a pastor, the darker side of their lives. It may be a discussion at Bible study or the casual conversation while you drive that triggers a memory. It may be another loss or a death that prompts the story to come forth. In my experience, the most profound sharing and listening moments in grief work have come in the unplanned and unexpected ways.

Serving Each Other

I have led many workshops on death and dying, loss and grief. While I prepared for a trip to a national women's conference in our denomination, at which I would lead a workshop about helping youth cope with loss and grief, I told our local women's group about the event and my plans. They were, as usual, very interested and supportive, even offering additional funds for travel and meals. After the meeting, the group's leader, Hazel, approached me privately and said she wanted to help me with my workshop and would like to visit with me about it sometime at my office. I said, "Great, let's set a time to get together."

The morning arrived. I met Hazel at the church office. We sat down and I simply said, "Tell me what's on your mind." She started to talk. She thought she was helping me with my workshop, but the conversation unlocked the secret she had kept for nearly sixty years. Hazel said, "I think helping children when someone dies is so important and it isn't done enough. Maybe my story will help you with your workshop. I don't want anyone to go through what I did."

For the next hour or more, Hazel told me the untold story about her silent grief. When she was a young teenager, she and her sister received a message at school that they should go home right away. No reasons or explanations were given. When they arrived home, their father, brother, and aunts were there, but silent. Finally the girls were told that their mother had died. Details were not shared. The young girls were told nothing, except not to worry, and not to talk about it with anyone. That was considered typical in this conservative, private Slovak family.

As the hours and days unfolded, Hazel did find out that her mother committed suicide and that her body had been discovered by her older brother. There was no

> **The truth that was hidden could not set her free.**

note and there were few clues as to her mother's reasons for taking her own life. There was great confusion and turmoil about the funeral and whether or not a church service would be permitted. With the encouragement and wise words of the local doctor, the priest consented. But that conflict, the silence and the shunning Hazel felt by those in the community and church, left its hurtful mark on her memory. She remembers other women in the family and church whispering to one another, only to stop when she and her siblings would enter the room. The children were left to themselves to imagine, wonder, and grieve alone.

As Hazel grew up, she tried to talk about her mother's death and her own grief, and to ask questions of her aunts—her mother's sisters. But again, this unexpected, untimely death by suicide was considered something that respectable Christian women did not discuss. For some time, she lived in her small community with a deep sense of embarrassment, with shame and judgment heaped upon her. And now, of course, her day-to-day activities had changed as well. A young teenage girl began sharing responsibilities of caring for a household with her sister. The child had not been allowed to grieve; and now she must become a woman with adult responsibilities and duties. She must be strong, keep her head held high, and her emotions hidden inside.

As months and years passed, she saw her brother withdraw into a world of silence and pain. His experience of grief was compounded when time and circumstances led him to serve his country during war. After his mother's death and the death and destruction he saw overseas, Hazel said he was never the same again, always living his life behind a cloud of silent sorrow.

Honoring with Trust

As for Hazel, she became a strong woman of faith with a family of her own. She knew hard work and the ups and downs of life. The generations passed away and fewer people knew of, and others forgot about, the significant events of her young life. From time to time, she wanted to talk with her husband and children about her life as a teenager and the sadness she still carried with her. With good intentions, they still gave her the message, "Don't talk about it because you become too upset." So she learned to live with the untold story and found ways to cope. She left the church of her childhood and became active in another congregation where her gifts of teaching the young, providing food and hospitality, and supporting other women have been her ministry.

I listened with awe to Hazel. I commented on the incredible length of time that had passed, and how she had been quiet about this burden of grief. I asked why she felt compelled to share it with me now.

She remarked that she was pleased to know that things are different now, at least for some children, when families experience death. She wanted people to be aware of the fear and pain that children and youth experience and how important it is to talk with their own children and grandchildren and to include them in the conversations of the family. Hazel said she knew of my interest in grief work; from the sermons I preached, she knew that I came from the vantage point of dealing with grief and death openly, as a matter of faith in a God of life. She trusted that she would be heard and that her experience would be respected. Hazel honored me with such trust.

Developing Their Gifts

Soon after I began serving congregations in the rural area of western Pennsylvania, I sought ways to communicate my concern about the impact that untold stories of unresolved grief play in people's lives. In building relationships and through preaching, Bible studies, small-group discussions, and visitation, I took the opportunity to give faith language to the loss and grief experiences of our lives as Christian people.

I have been amazed at the number of people (congregational members, and others who are relatives and friends) who have shared stories of grief, guilt, or fear that they have carried for so many years. Some said they knew that the church was a place to go in time of need, but had not found a pastor who had given them the level of trust needed to be so vulnerable. Many were afraid of further judgment and condemnation. Others held firmly to the cultural norm that you keep such important family matters private, no matter how much you may suffer from carrying the burden alone. Still others hold the belief that you must "get your act together first" and then show yourself as a worthy Christian person to the rest of the Church.

As ordinary as it may be, this has been a ministry of sharing and listening and connecting. I have shared pieces of my own story—the losses and disappointments, the healing and new purposes that have shaped my life as a woman of faith. Talking about depression, divorce, or death openly, and with words of understanding and grace, has opened the door for others to revisit the painful times of their lives with new perspective.

Hearing the real-life stories of Jean and Kay—two committed sisters—of Ellen, Hazel, and so many others has been a blessing in my ministry. Being a part of their stories of hope and healing strengthens my faith. These women, men, and children have been of tremendous help to me, and not only in preparation for grief workshops, but also in writing and preaching sermons. I am reminded that stories we are privileged to hear as ministers of the gospel are real, not just illustrations for sermons or even narrations for books. The whole of people's lives is entrusted to us when the conversations begin. In the listening and in the responding, God's presence is known and healing begins to happen.

Through the ministry of grief work, whether in ordinary conversation or in scheduled times of counseling, we share the gospel of Christ. Like cold water to the thirsty or food for the hungry, a listening ear and a word of comfort bring good news to a weary soul. Pastoral care includes listening, consoling, and sharing Christ's word of liberation to those who are bound by grief. I believe it also includes helping others discover their gifts for ministry in daily life so they can use the experiences of their lives and their abilities in ways that bring Christ's word and spirit of freedom to others in need.

In the ministry of grief work, we listeners can discover that those with stories to tell can bring good news to their friends, family, and neighbors in times of loss and grief. By being present and listening, by allowing the painful stories to be told, and by withholding unsolicited advice or condemnation, we are all ministers of hope. Because we have known tragedy or suffering and because the Holy Spirit has guided us through such times, we can be witnesses to the power of healing and wholeness, even in the midst of the grief that we may still carry.

It is in the loss, grief, death, and dying events of life and in the process of healing and finding life again, that we come to know in a most personal way, the power of death and resurrection.

CHAPTER THREE

Ordinary Priorities: The Ministry of Spiritual Direction

Holly W. Whitcomb

Who tells you who you are? In the quest to carry out the responsibilities of our many roles of personal relationships and public ministry, we can almost lose ourselves. Who can serve as pastor, mentor, confidant, confessor, or spiritual guide to the minister? Listen to Holly's story. Listen to your own heart, and listen to those who tell us how to listen once again to God.

It is believed that many centuries ago, Lao-tzu said, "Be really whole and all things will come to you." Ever since I was ordained twenty years ago, I have struggled with issues of balance: balance between family and job, between required work responsibilities and unrealistic expectations of work, between my own driven need for perfection and what I have come to call "good enoughness." When I have found myself trying arduously to climb out of the valley of dry bones, worn out and withered, I ask myself the question God asked Ezekiel: Can these bones live?

In the years I served as a parish pastor, my self-expectation went presumptuously off the charts. I worked obsessively so that no one would dare criticize me. Although I was a well-liked and respected pastor, no one knew the tired desperation of those years. I was a perfectionistic class act on the outside and an insecure bag of weary bones on the inside. My care of small children, my care of a congregation, my care of a physician husband with a demanding schedule of his own was too

> I could never work hard enough or please enough people.

much for me to handle. I eventually developed recurrent migraines in which I would temporarily lose half my vision. (Was God trying to tell me that I was literally losing sight of what was important?) My own self-projection told me I could never work hard enough or please enough people. I allowed myself to live fearfully and remained outer-directed, rarely allowing the Angel of Grace to draw near. I was God's cheerleader who had lost her cheer.

During my years of parish ministry, I served both as a solo pastor and as an associate pastor in several different congregations. Some obvious signs of disequilibrium included the following:

- public humiliation when neighbors called to tell me my son didn't need to keep standing out there waiting for the school bus because there was no school today. The last of these phone calls was the crumbling point when I realized I couldn't keep all the pots on all the burners boiling on high.
- nagging depression over the unrelenting attacks of one parish antagonist. I was too insecure to realize this was one individual and not a whole army.
- belief for a while that I must be the crazy one in a codependent congregation that colluded in keeping dysfunctional secrets in its leadership. During this time I sought help and clarity from the church hierarchy, but they, too, did not want to challenge the status quo.

An Ordinary Question and a Simple Directive

Minister: heal thyself. I have taken these words to heart. My own unwitting plunge into imbalance summoned me to seek a cure and has eventually allowed me to become an empathetic teacher of balance to others. When I invite others out of their valleys of dry bones, I ask not only the question, "Can these bones live?" but, "What is making these bones dry?" and "How can these bones learn to walk upright and someday even dance for joy?"

A first pivotal insight into my own need for balance dawned in the early 1980s during a national anti-nuclear conference at which William Sloane Coffin offered a keynote address. Coffin said that whenever we are required to determine where our conscience lies or what authority we will obey, we must first answer the question, "Who tells you who you are?" My answer to this question was a monumental revelation. When I first asked myself this question, my answer was "everybody." During ensuing years I thankfully can say that I have become more selective. Whenever each of us struggles honestly with this question, a sense of balance is restored. We can see more distinctly which are our true voices of authority and which are our false voices that seduce us by dallying with our egos and our lack of self-esteem. My grappling with this question, "Who tells you who you are?" was my first invitation to stop trying to be all things to all people.

A second dramatic insight into my own need for balance took place seven years ago when I attended a parenting seminar offered during adult education hour at our church. Knowing that I needed all the help I could get, I had looked forward to this parenting seminar and eagerly showed up at the class, pencil and paper in hand. I was convinced I would fill page after page with user-friendly tips and how-tos. Instead, the teacher elaborated the entire time on one simple directive: "What your children will inherit from you is your state of mind." Well, I wanted to run home and lock myself in a closet. What a stunning and terrifying thought. Unfortunately, how indubitably true. I returned home that day intent upon improving my daily state of mind. I have discovered that when I don't live with a self-nurturing, compassionate, and hopeful state of mind, my family and friends bear the brunt of my burnout: my guilt, my disillusionment, my resentment, and my fatigue. Taking what I have come to call "my personal weather report," an assessment of my current state of mind, continues to be a good navigational instrument out of the valley of dry bones.

A Ministry of Deepening Faith and Restoring Balance

The move in the last ten years from parish pastor to spiritual guide has been a life-giving choice for me, a choice that has suited my independent spirit well. Now that I am self-employed I am less of an ingratiating people-pleaser and I have more control over my weekly schedule. I take delight in the freedom, diversity, and ecumenical nature of my work.

In my present ministry as a retreat leader, spiritual director, and writer, I relish the role of spiritual midwife. It is deeply satisfying to help usher in the birth of revived faith, of increased self-esteem, of discernment and clarity, of trust in God's leading. In my role as spiritual director, I work with both clergy and laypeople who seek to follow God's guiding spirit to wholeness. In my retreat work with persons of all denominations, I provide participants with "a quiet place to rest awhile" as they gain new perspective on their relationship with themselves and with God. In my writing, I frequently design retreats and spirituality events that combine elements of spiritual autobiography and personal prayer, the practice of one's spiritual path and self-nurture, and the discovery of one's gifts and the response to God's call. My ministry, with God's help, is that of deepening faith and restoring balance.

I wear many hats in my life, as do most of us. I am a parent of teenage children, a clergywoman, a wife, a spiritual director, a writer, a cook, a soccer mom, and a school volunteer. Sometimes in spite of remembering all my helpful mantras and aphorisms, I still get stressed out and don't cope. I need a prayer life that offers me perspective, calm, and daily renewal.

How do I keep myself in balance? I share here a spiritual resource that has provided me with perspective. I rely on this daily inventory to offer me sanity, stability, and a sense of reconnection with God's grace. The awareness examen or inventory, known by various names (daily examen, examination of conscience, or even better, examination of consciousness) is an ancient and reputable tool. The practice of the examen became especially popular through Ignatius of Loyola (1495–1556) in his *Spiritual Exercises*. This daily inventory that I created for myself offers me a framework for reflection and prayer twice a day, once in the morning and once at night.

Morning Questions to Start the Day

1. *What is my intention for this day—how do I wish to conduct myself?*
I put a great deal of credence in the idea of intentionality: laying out our intentions for each new day. We have choices in how we will conduct ourselves, whether we will be petty, cantankerous, and vengeful, or whether we will choose to live with charity, non-judgement, and kindness. This question reminds me daily that I have choices in my behavior and that these choices are bound to impact the quality of my family life and of all my relationships.

2. *How might God be asking me to let go?*
I added this question recently because I was having a difficult time with some control issues. I can be a controlling person and my natural inclination is to manage everyone else's business. This question helps to free me of this tendency and to name concrete issues, situations, and persons that I need to release.

3. *Where do I seek God's wisdom and guidance?*
I pray for general guidance here ("God, guide my life") as well as for discernment about specific turning points, decisions, dilemmas, or conflicts. I also use this time to enter into prayers of intercession for the heal-

ing, comfort, and guidance of loved ones, friends, and brothers and sisters around the world.

Evening Questions to End the Day

1. *What have been my sources of grace this day—for what do I give thanks?*

This question allows me to see God's love moving in the small, but significant events of each day: a word of affirmation, an unexpected insight, a lovely bird or plant. We can cultivate the discipline and attitude of living in thanksgiving, rather than in discontent and deprivation. This naming of the day's often commonplace, but remarkable graces moves me in this direction.

2. *For what do I repent?*

There is always plenty of grist for the mill here, and I often feel ashamed and embarrassed; it helps me, however, to name it, claim it, and then move on. Since a true act of repentance always involves an accompanying change of heart, I feel cleansed and encouraged after I ask this question. Through this act of repentance, I reaffirm that I am not condemned to repeat thoughtless, selfish, or misguided acts over and over again.

This is the awareness examen, the daily inventory I created for me. I rely on its flexibility that I can omit certain questions or add pertinent new ones at any time. Others may want to reflect on their own spiritual challenges and create their own daily inventory. This prayerful inventory helps to keep me out of the valley of dry bones, and lets me know, in the words of Henri Nouwen, that I am God's beloved. It reminds me that grace is alive and well and being offered to me each and every day. It is an insightful form of prayer that has helped me to keep balance.

CHAPTER FOUR

Ordinary Water: Ministry Beyond Judgment

Mary Jo Maass

Where is God? Where does one find the water of life? Where is God's judgment? God's righteousness? God's mercy? How deep is our trust? How deep is God's well? How deep is God's trust? These are ministry questions as we are led to a community outside the walls of the church.

The woman invited Blandina into her home and offered her a cup of tea. She had heard about Blandina, a Christian who was visiting the women in the village. The woman was suspicious and curious. How was it that this churchwoman was coming to talk with the women of Kiboroloni? Over tea they began to share their stories.

A Samaritan woman came to draw water, and Jesus said to her, "Give me a drink." . . . The Samaritan woman said to him, "How is it that you, a Jew, ask a drink of me, a woman of Samaria?" (John 4:7, 9)

One Thing in Common

Kiboroloni is a small village in northern Tanzania, built on a slope in the foothills of Mount Kilimanjaro. Kiboroloni is famous as a marketplace and attracts buyers and traders from all over; it is unique in that its driving force is women.

Most of the women of Kiboroloni were not born there, but moved there

40

from various tribes and villages throughout Tanzania. They have one thing in common—they came in the midst of crisis or desperation. They came with the hope of making a new life for themselves and their children. Together they drank the waters of Kiboroloni and became successful, confident, and independent. Rumor has it that they become rich through

> ## The church seemed without a bucket, and the well was deep.

such suspect activities as smuggling, prostitution, and producing home-brew *(mbege)*.

I became acquainted with Kiboroloni through my friend and classmate, Blandina, at Makumina Theological College. I visited her several times to get the feel of the village, the women, and the church. I was intrigued by these village women who had common roots with their neighbors, yet were separated, looked down upon and despised by them. Blandina was writing her thesis on the women of Kiboroloni and the church's ministry to them. As the year unfolded, she shared her story with me.

> [Jesus] had to go through Samaria. So he came to a Samaritan city called Sychar, near the plot of ground that Jacob had given to his son Joseph. Jacob's well was there, and Jesus, tired out by his journey, was sitting by the well. It was about noon. A Samaritan woman came to draw water. . . .
> (John 4:4-7*a*)

Blandina had to pass through Kiboroloni on the way to completing her degree. The women came to drink the waters of Kiboroloni to sustain their life. Slowly, through the sharing of their stories, Blandina came to know all about them.

The women were of various ages and educational levels. They came from near and far. They came fleeing forced marriages or the threat of circumcision. They came from marriages broken by death, abuse, or childlessness. Some came with their children; others had to leave their children behind. One woman, abandoned because of a childless marriage, gave birth to three children as a single parent in Kiboroloni. Another had tried to make a living for herself in other villages before someone advised her to come here. They came in desperation to drink the waters of Kiboroloni.

The women helped each other to become established. They had small farms and sold their extra produce at market. Soon they had small shops where they sold used clothing or *kitangas* and *kongas*. It was important to have more than one source of income, because you never knew when or where the business winds would blow. Women with little education could make more money in business than educated women could make teaching school. These women succeeded. They controlled their own money; they made their own decisions. They sent their children to school. They were quenching their thirst from the waters of Kiboroloni—a well with enough water for all.

> Jesus answered her, "If you knew the gift of God, and who it is that is saying to you, 'Give me a drink,' you would have asked him, and he would have given you living water." The woman said to him, "Sir, you have no bucket, and the well is deep. Where do you get that living water?
>
> (John 4:10-11)

Living Worship

Blandina told the women, "You worship what you do not know; we worship what we know, for salvation is from the church." The women answered her, "When we hold positions of leadership in the church, people from the other churches in the diocese complain that we are not fit leaders."

One single mother explained, "I would like to come for communion, but when I became pregnant I was put under church discipline. I could not take communion until after the child was born and I had confessed my sins to the congregation and had been accepted back into the church. Now, I am pregnant again. It is easier not to go to communion. But, I go to worship and I send my children to Sunday school and confirmation." Another woman reminded Blandina that Sunday was a good market day. She had no one to help her; she could not afford to close her shop.

> The woman said to him, "Sir, I see that you are a prophet. Our ancestors worshiped on this mountain, but you say that the place where people must worship is in Jerusalem." (John 4:19-20)

The women Blandina talked with knew that Jesus was their Savior and that he was with them in all things. They worshiped on the slopes of Kiboroloni in all that they did. Wasn't it Jesus who had brought them to drink the waters of Kiboroloni?

Prayer Groups, Projects, and Programs

Over the next few months, Blandina compiled her data, wrote the stories of the women, and reflected on the implications of her research. She shared her reflections with me. The church had implemented many programs to minister to these women. There were Bible studies and prayer groups. There were educational seminars on marriage and family, child care and nutrition. There were lectures on church discipline and the dangers of alcohol and immoral living. There were projects, too, to help the women earn extra money.

But now that Blandina knew these women, she could see that the programs did not fit them. These women had been abused severely, some barely escaping with their lives. None of them wanted to marry or become dependent again. What good were seminars on marriage and family life? What good was church discipline when it disciplined only the mothers who became pregnant and not the fathers? What good were projects to replace the brewing of *mbege* that did not bring in enough money to support these women and their children? Could the church support them, make their decisions for them, give them children? Could the church give these women the water of life? The church seemed without a bucket and the well was deep. Where do we find living water?

> But the hour is coming, and is now here, when the true worshipers will worship the Father in spirit and truth, for the Father seeks such as these to worship him. . . . The woman said to him, "I know that Messiah is coming" (who is called Christ). "When he comes, he will proclaim all things to us." Jesus said to her, "I am he, the one who is speaking to you."   (John 4:23, 25-26)

Quietly and hesitantly Blandina spoke, "Maybe the church should accept and encourage these women. Maybe it is the church that is in crisis. Maybe it is the church who needs these women to minister to us. If we struggle together, maybe we can find the life-giving water in Kiboroloni for all of us."

That is the end of Blandina's story of the women of Kiboroloni. There seems to be more than one story here—the lines become blurred. Where is Jesus in this story? I thought Blandina was Christlike, coming from the church with the water of life for the women. But now I see Jesus in the women of Kiboroloni, sharing their stories and giving each other (and the church) the water of life.

Somehow, in the sharing of the story, in the sharing of the water, life has been changed—the lines have become blurred. A community has been born out of the waters, one that supports, accepts, and ministers to one another. They have all become the Body of Christ. In that community there is hope; the spring of water gushes up and there is new life.

I have drunk from these waters. I have become a part of the story, a part of the community of Blandina, these women, and the church. And so have you.

> "[Jesus said] but those who drink of the water that I will give them will never be thirsty. The water that I will give will become in them a spring of water gushing up to eternal life." (John 4:14)

CHAPTER FIVE

Ordinary Apathy: The Ministry of Challenge

Kris Ann Zierke

Incorporation in the Body of Christ empowers this "unincorporated" community to move beyond its limited self-image. Ministerial opportunities often arise in crisis, but crisis doesn't necessarily lead to ministry. Can a whole congregation come to trust God, to trust themselves to be what God is transforming them to become? To know they exist for ministry of providential concern for their community

This is the story of how extraordinary events, and a congregation's response to them, had the power to transform ministry. I serve a two-point parish in Adams County, Wisconsin. Trinity Church is a small congregation in the city of Adams. Zion Church of Big Flats is an extremely small church in a small unincorporated community, with eighty-five baptized members. Zion had an average worship attendance of about thirty-five when I arrived. In the "town," there are a couple of bars, a restaurant, town hall, potato fields, and homes. County Highway C runs past the town hall, and so could be considered "Main Street." Zion was not very different from most congregations, and it suffered from a common disease: apathy. The members were good people committed to their congregation, but not knowing what that meant within the larger community. A crisis transformed both the community and the congregation forever.

The Tornado

In August of 1994, on a Saturday night, only thirteen months after I came to Adams County as pastor, a tornado swept through the town of Big Flats. The tornado followed a path along Highway C, zigzagging first to the north side of the road and then the south. Everything in its path was devastated, but on its erratic course, one home might be destroyed while the one next door was left untouched. A bar, the town hall, and many homes were destroyed. Trees were toppled. Two people were killed. The National Guard was called out; the Salvation Army was there to help; volunteers from Adams County and a nearby community who had suffered a tornado several years before were there to help clean up.

The people of Zion Congregation were extremely fortunate. There were only a few families who had minor damage to their homes; the church building was unscathed, although the tornado passed within a half mile of it. The people of the congregation, grateful that they had been spared, were not complacent. Their neighbors, some they had known all their lives and some strangers, were in need. Immediately after an abbreviated worship service the next day, the members of the congregation set out with chain saws, eager to help their neighbors. Indeed, some had already been out most of the night working with the fire department to make sure that those injured were found.

The Challenge

By Monday afternoon, the Inter-Lutheran Disaster Agency had responded to the emergency by giving the congregation a check for $5,000 to help in the clean-up efforts. Now the challenge began. How would the money be used? Who would determine who would receive the money and what would be done with it? The congregation members looked for guidance in ways to help. It was decided that the pastor and the secretary would canvass the neighborhood to see what kind of help was needed. The Salvation Army was providing temporary trailers for those whose homes had been destroyed, but no assistance had been offered for the cost of gas and electrical hookups. So some of the money was used to provide electric and well hookups. A trailer of furniture, clothing, and household goods arrived from Michigan. We tried to give things away, notifying people as we spoke with them about what was

> *They could make their dream come true when it became a dream for their community.*

available. No one would take our "charity. " Finally, we decided to hold a rummage sale. All the goods were sold at very low prices, and the money was poured back into the disaster relief fund. People flocked to the rummage sale, some who had tornado damage, some who did not. This particular community is a very poor rural area—if there is such a thing as a rural slum, this is it. The rummage sale benefited those poorer people in the community who did not have tornado damage, as well as those who did.

Zion also helped with the cleanup. The tornado had traveled eastward along highway C, crossing a state highway. Most of the other relief effort was concentrated east of the state highway near the town hall, so we worked west of the highway. We advertised throughout our synod and received help from far away. The owner of a waste disposal company in a town about ninety miles away brought a Dumpster and truck to help us. We cleared branches, cement, glass, and other debris from yards and the road. The congregation held a picnic for the community so that people might share stories, frustrations, and joys. In the spring, we gave away trees to replace those lost to the tornado; signs of hope and rebuilding. In all, this tiny congregation was given stewardship of $22,000 from congregations, individuals, and communities. All of our relief efforts were "ordinary" things, filling common, ordinary needs of people in the community, aimed at returning people to normal life.

The Dream

Today, there are still signs of the tornado—trees that are not cleared away, homes destroyed and not rebuilt. This small community will never be the same again. And neither will the congregation. Before the tornado, Zion was a typical "family chapel," several families related to one another keeping the congregation going but not growing. They were good, faithful people, concerned with surviving, but lacking a sense of mission. But they did have a dream—really a wish. The church building had no indoor plumbing, no kitchen or meeting facility. Members had begun slowly saving to build an addition, complete with indoor bathrooms, a kitchen, and a meeting room.

What the tornado did for this congregation was nothing short of miraculous. The wind blew through the community and showed the people of Zion that they existed for a real purpose in this place and at that time. They saw that people had needed them, that this money would not have gotten to the community without the hard work and the presence of their congregation in its midst. They saw, perhaps for the first time, that they had something tangible and important to offer the community: the love and compassion of God, the gospel, in word and deed.

This congregation, whose vision had only been to keep the doors open another year, began to look for ways to reach out into the community. The Christmas food boxes, a long-standing project of the congregation, were increased that year. Zion provided help to families who needed clothes and food after household fires. They began inviting their neighbors to attend church, and membership increased. Their dream of building began to seem like a possibility, and then even a necessity. This not-so-subtle shift in thinking, begun as a wish born out of wearied tramping to the out-house on cold winter days, became a desire to serve the community. People were heard to say, "We need to build this addition so that we can do more in the community."

After four long years of fund-raising, the congregation decided to pursue the project. They hired an architect to draw up the plans, and a contractor supervised the building. The congregation worked hard raising money, but also did most of the work themselves. In April of 1998, nearly four years after the tornado, Zion dedicated its new facility. They added on to the original building an office, kitchen, fellowship hall, two bathrooms, and a basement for storage, all built debt free. The tornado had stirred this congregation's imagination and their spirit, teaching them that they could make their dream come true, when it became a dream for their community.

While still basking in the glow of our success, the challenge laid before the congregation is to continue to grow in the understanding of our mission, of that which we have to offer to our community. What is next for us, we are not sure. We do know that as we seek to be faithful to God's mission for us, spreading the good news in our community, God will continue to challenge and surprise us, to stretch us beyond what we ever thought possible.

CHAPTER SIX

Ordinary Process: The Ministry of Administration

Kathryn K. J. Gerking

A story within a story, Kathy tells Barbara's story and goes beyond to tell her own. How can we understand the inscrutable will of God? How does one ever know what God is doing here? And what is our role in the midst of it all? We are called to faithful, courageous leadership, trusting in the God who is Providence, Provider, and Patient One.

I saved the voice mail for weeks, long after the response had been made and the need tended to:

"Hello Kathy? This is Pastor Barbara Bullock-Tiffany. Um, I'm just calling to say that I've had more health issues develop and I may need you to preach and maybe preside on Reformation Sunday. I've arranged for the Intern Pastor at a local church to take this Sunday's service, but I'm not sure what will happen this next week and wondered if you could be available? It's our confirmation service. Please give me a call or I'll call you later. We're heading in for some tests soon. . . ."

"I'm not sure what will happen next week." Particularly true for this pastor, but also true for all of us in life and in ministry. The work to which I am presently called is to assist the ministry of the office of the bishop. I understood my call to be one of supporting and strengthening leaders of congregations and pastors for ministry and mission in their parishes and institutions. Many days bring a phone call or an E-mail communicating a new reality, a new need, or another idea to pursue. In some ways, these

49

are like the blessed "interruptions" of parish ministry, for they give shape to the ways in which I might offer support and encouragement to my colleagues in ministry and to the church. They also challenge me as I make decisions about which call needs my response first. Which nice idea will I pursue next? When might I find time to research the response to that question I have not encountered before?

A Bittersweet Privilege

With Pastor Barbara's phone call, the priority was clear. Issues of life and death always take precedence in this office, just as in the parish. Two days after first receiving the voice mail, I was spending some time with Barbara at the local university hospital. The anxious moments that had begun with illness during Holy Week, and intensified during the summer, now were looming again. What was going on with her body? Surgery was no longer an option; could there be a different chemotherapy that would help? What will she say to her three-year-old? These are the same questions that many forty-year-old women sift through at times of crisis; but for this pastor, the added dimension of serving her parish was in her thoughts.

It is a bittersweet privilege to walk with people in such moments of challenge and hope. My visits were often at the end of my work day, which happened to be when Barbara's husband, Doug, also a pastor, would leave the hospital to pick up their son from child care arrangements. Barbara and I spent some hours on those evenings discussing her parish ministry. *"We've really made some progress in this. . . . I'm trying to "give away" the responsibility in this area; though it is something I really enjoy, I know others can do it. . . . I'm really challenged by how to deal with some people. . . . What do you do when. . . . ? I enjoy confirmation ministry, especially the class that will be confirmed next year. I started with them, and we've developed some new patterns. They are certainly a lively bunch. I'm thinking that, once they are confirmed, I'll have a sense of completedness, in terms of the work I've been called to do in this congregation. Sometimes I wonder whether I might be called to pastoral and music ministry in some setting. . . ."*

This was "ordinary conversation" that I might have with any pastor evaluating work and ministry, looking for a sense of progress and lasting impressions of gifts given and received, discerning that holy sense of call. How is the wind of the Holy Spirit blowing in one's life? Where should one focus? Where might one pull back? This was also the "ordinary conversation" I might have with a young woman, wife, mother who is confident of God's providence and whose will to live is strong. *"If this chemotherapy does not work, we'll go to a cancer center. I've been reading about and trying alternative medicines. . . ."*

The days passed quickly. We located an "emergency" interim pastor to give Barbara some leave time; he could start on All Saints' Sunday. As Barbara requested, I arrived on the morning of Reformation Sunday to preside at the worship during which four ninth-grade youth would affirm their baptisms, and become confirmed members of the congregation.

I wore Pastor Barbara's red stole as we gathered in her office to meet and discuss the particulars of the service. The books were still open on her desk, the papers shuffled into stacks awaiting her attention. I thought of Barbara, like Paul, who had "fought the good fight," and run with perseverance the race that was set before her. In the last-minute phone calls, after she had proofread the bulletin for the service from her hospital room and called me to draw attention to a couple of mistakes, I sensed that I was being handed the baton in what needed now to become a relay race. *"After this Sunday, I can let go for awhile,"* she said, *"but I really want their confirmation to be special. If I can't be there, then I want the Assistant to the Bishop to lead them through the affirmation and pray for the Holy Spirit to be stirred up within them. . . ."*

> **As vision and discernment drive us forward, patience serves us well.**

Pastor Barbara Bullock-Tiffany was not to run any additional legs of the relay here on earth. In less than a month, I joined her family and her congregation in mourning our beloved sister in faith. I couldn't imagine that my colleague who was a gifted pastor, an energetic and talented musician, a loving mother and wife, and a joyful participant in life was so quickly gone. I remember thinking on the day of the funeral that God had surely made some irreversible mistake in our midst. Perhaps it is the very nature of such tragedy that keeps me even now from reflecting upon it with understanding. There is only, finally, acceptance.

Purposeful Journeys, Patience in Process

"We know that all things work together for good for those who love God, who are called according to his purpose." These words of Paul in Romans 8:28 are an invitation to come along in faith. Do we really *know* that all things work together for good? What are God's purposes for us? What is God's yearning for our lives? What is this sense of "call"? How might we share the confidence of "knowing" with Paul?

To claim that "all things work together" toward God's purposes is to believe that God's loving hands are shaping, molding, and uplifting us constantly, even in the midst of great challenges. It is not to make light of the sometimes difficult or desperate situations in which we find ourselves. It is not the same as "blessing" our own mistakes, or glossing over faults and troubles. It is the gift of faith that trusts that the power of God is at work with the broken, rough, and sharp-edged pieces of our lives. God's power gives us the courage to continue seeking ways of being there for one another and improving our common witness and faithfulness.

Most of my time these days is spent in empowering the ministry in daily life of pastors and others who serve in the church. Mostly, I provide counsel for people in the midst of processes (some longing for stability, others seeking change): call processes, congregational conflict processes, area ministry study processes. I have commonly come to repeat this refrain to myself: *In the timing is the Spirit*. As vision and discernment drive us forward, patience serves us well. Panic, or other reasons for quick decisions, sometimes will lead us to harvest unripened fruit. It is often very difficult to wait to sift issues through in processes that can sometimes seem endless. The words of Isaiah 40:31 are apt encouragement for the perspective of patience: "Those who wait upon the LORD shall renew their strength, they shall mount up with wings like eagles, they shall run and not be weary, they shall walk and not faint."

One congregation had worked through a particularly long and focused interim between pastorates. After about one year, colleagues from the office of the bishop, who preceded me, began to work with the congregation in a call process. It seemed that I would reap the fruit of their labor, for shortly after I began, I was pleased to conduct a congregational call meeting and to work with their candidate on the final steps. The call was issued, accepted, and an installation date set. However, just days prior to moving, the pastor resigned from this call for personal reasons. We were all very disappointed.

Within a few days, the bishop and I were part of a joint meeting of the congregation's council and the call committee. Together we processed our disappointment, tried to understand the situation, and made provisions for the next steps. Following the meeting, a woman came to me and said, "I wouldn't say this in front of everybody, but I don't think we were really ready to receive a new pastor yet. When it's God's timetable, and not ours, our pastor will come." I was perplexed by the perspective but heartened by her insight. The call committee and I worked diligently for another ten months until a pastor was called.

I remembered the woman's comment in the days when the call committee became frustrated with the time it took to arrange for interviews and for some pastors to make pertinent decisions. At one point, the committee considered "moving ahead with one of these candidates" because the process had been so long, their interim pastor was now gone, and at least one of the candidates wouldn't be available until what seemed to be many months down the road. "If urgency weren't a driving issue," I asked, "which person do you believe God is calling to be your pastor as you write the next chapter of ministry together? That should be the focus of your next committee meeting." Such prayerful, patient, discernment processes can be urged because we are trusting God to provide for our needs along the way. The congregation, by the way, finally and joyfully called and received a pastor.

The woman's evaluation of "readiness" may or may not have been accurate. It was a perspective appropriately only discerned from within the congregation; not an evaluation I would have ventured as an outsider. But it was an encouraging reminder to me. It helped me counsel patience and trust in God's provisions when the call process might have been otherwise seized by frustration or urgency.

Trust and Discernment

Even though I urge patience in the midst of process, I believe that sometimes holy impatience and indignation are properly warranted responses. Although I urge people to trust God to lead and guide them through a process, I also know that some processes are unfocused or essentially flawed. I know that God can work through any flawed process, but I also believe that many processes within the church can and should be examined and improved. I find it essential to work patiently with both perspectives: seek to change the system as needed while participating with patience and the confidence that God works through our brokenness.

Again and again, I see examples of God's work with us in times of seeking direction and working through processes. Looking back with this perspective, I would claim my own experience of waiting for a pastoral call as such a time. I was ordained three and a half years after I was available to the church for call. Due to some decisions made by others, and some made by my husband and me, I became a "geographically restricted" pastoral candidate. These were three blessed, enriching, and sometimes frustrating years during which I experienced the church from an "in but not of" perspective. I sometimes felt like the Canaanite woman begging for crumbs from the table, longing for someone to "just tell me where I stand" and persistently questioning my bishop's assistant about "what might be next."

Yet I gained valuable experience in those years. I served part-time in several positions: teaching confirmation, teaching Old and New Testament at a local college, doing pastoral supply work (in some pulpits one of the first women to preach), even by working as a secretary in a legal office! We moved four times in those years, in order not to make housing commitments that would further tie us down.

These were not always easy months. My geographical limitation meant that I was sometimes a candidate in processes where congregations were looking for more experience, or even in congregations that were predisposed against calling a woman as their pastor. I struggled with my own sense of call, and I learned immensely with each opportunity, challenge, or disappointment. The time of waiting also afforded me the opportunity to focus on my young marriage and my newborn daughter, to understand family considerations as being also a part of God's gift of vocation for me.

God shaped me uniquely during that time with experiences that inform and affect my work today. The variety of those roles, with their calls to patience and impatience in ways not always understood at the time, prepared me for ministry in the bishop's office. Just as a person preparing a meal for many guests has lots of kettles on the stove and projects on the counter, a synod office tends a lot of processes. Some are unusual and demanding. Many of them routine, bureaucratic, mundane, and ordinary. It is sometimes only as we look back on them that we see the extraordinary unfolding grace of the Holy Spirit, Comforter, Advocate, and Guide.

"I'm not sure what will happen next week," Barbara Bullock-Tiffany had said to me. Yet even in the midst of the personal uncertainty, this pastor sought out a way to complete a process she had begun with some young people, to accompany them to a milestone on their spiritual journey. We do not see clearly how God is at work in such moments, even if we practice patience and trust God's timing. Sometimes life and death intervene, bringing us to decision points and ultimately altering our path. This is the case for Pastor Barbara's family and for the congregation she had served so well. Now the interim pastor leads an intentional grief process in that congregation. The congregation is working to publish a book that will include some of her music and some of her homilies. While being patient with each other they journey through this process they would not have chosen, trusting God to lead, direct, and bless.

For now we see in a mirror, dimly, but then we will see face to face. Now I know only in part; then I will know fully, even as I have been fully known (1 Corinthians 13:12).

PART TWO
LIBERATING CHRISTIANS

Christian ministry arises from Christ's incarnation, life, death, and resurrection. We are called to ministries of reconciliation, freedom, rebirth, and new life. Jesus put on flesh; therefore, our ministry needs to put on flesh. Christ was born in the most common of all places, a feed box in a stall. His birth, in an out-of-the-way place, was very ordinary. No one had room for him in that town. Nor did he neatly fit into the religious confines of his day. He came to set us free, even from our own religiosity.

Jesus ministered among the outcasts. He met people where they were, on the road, in their life situations. We are called to ministries of incarnation, visiting people where they are. He listened and healed, and spoke of righteousness and justice. The one who had no place to lay his head was always calling us home. We who have been plunged into his death and resurrection in our baptism are invited to be part of Christ's very body. We, who are called ministers in the name of Jesus, are empowered to proclaim and live justice-seeking, life-giving good news in the public world.

Christ's ministry among us liberates us to participate in Jesus' ongoing liberating ministries. He is always already in that place to which we are called. He is always on the other side of any barrier human beings might erect. We have been called to leave behind our own fears and false gods so that we might minister in wholeness of life to people as we walk with them in ordinary places of daily life.

The Christian life begins in baptism. In this individualistic, mobile society, ministers often receive a request to "baptize my grandchild," who is "home" for the weekend. But baptism is not merely a family occasion, nor just a one-time event. Our first story begins with Barbara Knutson facing the theological and communal dilemmas of such a request. Should she acquiesce? Moving beyond a "yes" or "no" answer," neither dismissing nor judging, she plunged the community into creative ministry. They took the request from those on the periphery not less, but more seriously. Baptism is important, not because it "takes care of things" by satisfying family wishes, but because it connects us with Jesus Christ and therefore with one another in the Body of Christ. When a request for ministry is outside our context, beyond our "responsibility," how can we broaden the concept of church? How do we move beyond request for ministry of personal convenience to communal care?

When Mary Rowland received the invitation to consider writing for this book, she was going out the door, to prison. Her story takes us along, to visit parishioners there. We see ministries of visitation, organization, and demonstration for justice, all of it liberating ministry. We, too, are called to engage in Christ's ministry in prison. From what are we to be liberated in our communal quest for justice? This call requires long commitment; it is ministry that one cannot engage in alone, so Mary is part of a coalition. This is what liberating Christians do: they spend their lives on behalf of the oppressed. "Ordinary Courage" may seem like an oxymoron, but courage dare not be a momentary, heroic, one-time occurrence (any more than baptism is). We need to cultivate the habit of justice. Each of us, open to Christ's liberating work of life over death, of freedom over bondage, will be led to a place that requires courage.

A surprising number of stories in this volume include ministry in the face of death. We who engage in parish ministry cannot avoid the subject of that ultimate reality. But if the Christian message is about anything, it is about the sure hope of the resurrection. A mother and daughter, both seminary graduates, wrote the next chapter together, an intergenerational dialogue, echoing intergenerational ministry. Their narrative moves us to listen to stories beyond the present congregational membership. How do we listen to the stories of those who are buried in the country churchyard? Their stories still teach the young children who play there of God's steady, constant love. The heart of the gospel is hope. Karen Rask Behling and Carol Rask lead us to specific ways we can share this liberating news across generations, thereby not only "studying church history" but living and recording it.

Bishop April Ulring Larson reminds us that at the heart of the Cross and Resurrection are reconciliation and resulting companionship. The women at the open tomb were told to "go and tell" that Jesus would meet the disciples in Galilee—even those who could not watch with him, or those who had denied him (Mark 16:7). Jesus did not proclaim himself "home free" as we in our individualistic competitive society might do. The gospel is that human beings are joined with the death and resurrection of Jesus and therefore joined to one another in ways that no one can separate. April's story is about receiving ministry from a brother bishop and about the ministry of companionship that moves from care to action. It is also a story about companion synods and their bishops who grew to be friends, thereby leading us all toward actions of justice in an inequitable world. How do we talk about Jesus in such a way that we keep listening? We may learn how from those who know better than we about principalities and powers, and about subsequent suffering. How important to cherish daily life, and the companions we receive when Jesus meets us as friends.

Part of pastoral work is the ministry of preaching. But sermon preparation and delivery are not isolated from other ministry, nor should they be isolating. We cannot begin to know the power of the pulpit until it connects with people's ordinary lives. Ginger Anderson-Larson's story begins with a letter from her niece. She is tempted to set it aside for the "more important" task of sermon preparation, until she realizes it is an entrée to the text. Christian ministry rarely entails just one task at a time. Effective preachers listen to the text and to the context and use their vantage point of leadership to connect preaching, education, outreach, and evangelism. How does the gospel of Christ's resurrection touch the contemporary world? When might our radical ministry reach the front page of the daily newspaper? In a society in which faith communities are seen as belonging to the private sphere, such opportunities for public proclamation may seem rare. Need they be? This story may invite us to seize the moment.

Jesus met people on the road. In this final chapter of Part Two, Norma Cook Everist, a seminary professor, goes on the road to visit and learn from seminary graduates in their ordinary daily routines. Likewise, pastors, diaconal ministers, and laity are called to walk with the people of God carrying out their ministries in daily life. In the ministry of pastoral visitation, how can one enter another's life without being an intruder? How do we visit another's location without being merely a tourist? How can we see what they see? How do we help them gain perspective, interpret their contexts, and reflect theologically on the challenges they face? The themes of Scripture and tenets of theology are right there in front of us, not neatly arranged in systematic order, but ready for inductive study. We drive with Norma and see the church and its ministry. We visit old white-frame church buildings and modern mission structures. We explore contrasting contexts, but the same basic liturgy—very different neighborhoods but the same Body of Christ.

CHAPTER SEVEN

Ordinary Request: The Ministry of the Baptismal Community

Barbara J. Knutson

It all begins in baptism. But it cannot end there, with that brief action at the font. How do we reach out and challenge people to see the radical thing they are doing for life? When adult children have moved on, and drifted away from regular worship, what does a pastor, and a congregation do to help them keep their baptismal promises?

"Pastor," she said, "my granddaughter from Pennsylvania is going to be contacting you. She and her husband have a baby they'd like you to baptize when they come to visit us in Minnesota. I just thought I'd let you know in advance."

Mabel sounded like one of those from the advance team of seventy sent out by Jesus. She is one of those salt-of-the-earth members of the congregation. At eighty, Mabel and her husband Henry have lived through enough of the changes of life to know what matters. Baptism matters. As their new pastor, I knew that too. So did the congregation's leaders.

Yet something gnawed at me as I reflected on Mabel's phone call. Could this be just another young couple who, out of respect for two elderly grandparents, want to have their child baptized? Who is this baptism for anyway?

Baptismal Promises

In the back of my mind I was thinking that the young couple's motivation might be askew. They might be more concerned about pleasing grandparents than about giving up their child for adoption. I wondered if they knew what this radical action of God means. In the sacrament of Holy Baptism, this child will be adopted by God. To belong to God and God's whole baptismal family is a serious life-changing matter. Life can never be the same.

To underscore my skeptical meanderings, Mabel told me that Jodi and Jon had another child, Matt, who also had been baptized in our congregation. That was six years ago. So where have they been the past six years? Where have they been with those baptismal promises to faithfully bring Matt to the services of God's house? Where have they been in the baptismal promises to teach him the stories of God and to pray? I found it hard not to be overcome by such obvious, yet ponderous questions.

> We embraced this request as a ministry opportunity.

Those questions needed to be asked. Because they were essential questions, they went deeper. Because they went deeper, they had significance for ministry. Their significance for ministry attacked my skepticism.

I began to ask "what-if" opportunity-for-ministry questions:

- What if the expected telephone call could enable this congregation and its leaders to remember our own baptisms?
- What if this expected request could shape us into modeling ministry that, in ordinary ways, would illuminate the extraordinary grace of God?
- What if this anticipated baptism would lead our congregation out beyond itself into wider connections with the one Body of Christ?
- What if, rather than doing long-distance diagnosis of a young family, we might embody what it means to be a baptismal community in Christ to them?
- What if God really means it: "As many of you as were baptized into Christ have clothed yourselves with Christ" (Galatians 3:27)?

A council meeting in this small membership, open-country congregation is like gathering around the family table. It's where we talk over matters of our life together.

By the time of the next monthly council meeting, Mabel's granddaughter,

Jodi, had called me. No, they had not affiliated with any congregation where they lived. And yes, it would be important to them to have their second child, Kelsey, also baptized in our church.

In this congregation, we speak often of the treasure we are given in Holy Baptism. The large oak octagonal-shaped baptismal font has a central place in the sanctuary. Each week as we gather to worship God, we begin where it all began for us, at the font. There we confess our brokenness and failure to love God and one another wholeheartedly. There, like refreshing rain to a parched earth, we are soaked in God's gracious forgiveness. Our preaching and teaching are baptismally anchored.

So together we embraced this request as a ministry opportunity. The Triune God, in whose name we baptize, would be here in full delight for Kelsey Eric on March 9. A new and joyful freedom came to us as we let God be the God of this baptism, too. (It never works anyway when we try to direct or control the grace of God!) We prayed to be able to hear how God wanted us to serve on this occasion.

Everything we did seemed so ordinary. We used the telephone and wrote letters. I sent the couple a copy of the baptismal service and invited their questions. Rather quickly, we sensed relationship with them. It felt like we knew Jodi, Jon, Matt, and Kelsey. A few of the council members remembered Matt's baptism. We were eager to meet them.

The ordinary, extraordinary Word of God in us and through us was, "Welcome. In God's name, welcome. And welcome to the family of God." The wind of God's Spirit energized us as we talked and planned together over the miles. Whether or not we could put words to it at the time, we were already celebrating the kingdom of God among us.

Communal Conversation

The day came for us to meet in person. Understandably the young family was tired. They had flown from Pennsylvania to Chicago. There they met their friend Mike, a young man in his 20s, who would be one of the sponsors. Together they drove the long trek from Chicago to southern Minnesota.

As we gathered in the living room of my parsonage that afternoon, there was no second-guessing their gladness over the beginning of Kelsey's new journey in Christ. Indeed, God was gifting us in this congregation. We were being blessed with the privilege of welcoming and shepherding another little one into Christ's "one, holy, catholic and apostolic church," which knows no boundaries of space or time.

Betty, the other sponsor, and a member of our sister congregation in this parish, joined us. As we lingered over the words and actions of the baptismal service, we marveled at God's mighty work. We were thrilled by our time together. The old liturgical words returned Mike to the refreshment of God's promises. His eyes sparkled. He came alive as he spoke of being nurtured in those promises in a childhood church in Iowa. The unconditional, irreversible love of God for us all on the journey was again what amazed us. We shared stories of where each of us had been in life. As we shared, we were in awe over how the God of our baptismal lives accepts us as we are, but never leaves us where we are! Indeed, our baptism means that the surprises of God will never cease. Pitfalls aplenty have been there, and will be there. Both delights and dangers accompany our sojourning. We admitted how we struggle with both the subtle and blatant temptations to live for ourselves. Kelsey would not be spared this either. So we pledged to pray for him and support him in his journey with us in faithfulness to the gospel. We promised to help him grow up in the faith, to help him know and love the God who claims him forever. But how will Kelsey know this? How will he know and believe that all of the promises of God find their "yes" in Christ? (2 Corinthians 1:20).

"Oh," we said, "that is our mission *together.*" *Together* is the word of the church. It is an empowering reality. God's Spirit does the work. And we keep telling one another what God is doing. God does the work of baptism into Christ. We come clothed, dressed up in Christ, and promise to never let one another forget the Christ of our life and salvation. Being Christ's baptismal community is our joy. Of such was our conversation that afternoon.

Being that community of grace meant something more. From the beginning, I had talked with Jodi and Jon about our eagerness to help them find a church home where they lived. So here we were, in my living room, huddling around a map of the eastern states. Kelsey's family home in southern Pennsylvania bordered Maryland and Delaware. We turned to our denomination's yearbook to find nearby congregations where they might be nourished for the next years of their baptismal life together.

Four congregations seemed to be geographically close: two in Pennsylvania, one in Delaware, and one in Maryland. Their data revealed interesting variety—which is always the picture of the Body of Christ. There seemed to be choices in membership size, programs, and ministry emphases. Names, addresses, telephone numbers, and the pastors' names were all jotted down on a piece of paper. The young couple expressed gratitude for this helpful encouragement to find a new church home.

Sacramental Celebration

The next day, the day we had longed for arrived. God's people were there. In Word and sacraments God was there. In the waters of baptism Kelsey was buried with Christ to be raised with Christ forever. And we became witnesses of these things!

Characteristic of all of God's children on the baptismal journey, Kelsey squirmed and kicked. But no amount of fussing on his or our part will ever stop the steadfast love of God for us. Kelsey will be told that along the way.

To remember this extraordinary day of grace, ordinary gifts were given to Kelsey, his parents, and sponsors. Wax, cloth, paper, seashells, and food are ordinary gifts of the earth. When connected to God's action, in a community of faith, the ordinary fascinates us with the extraordinary liveliness of God with us and for us.

One of the deacons lit a baptismal candle from the Paschal candle, a symbol of the light no darkness can quell. She gave the little candle to Kelsey's parents and gave baby Kelsey Jesus' words, "Let your light so shine before others that they may see your good works and glorify your Father in heaven." These were big words for a little one. There's a lifetime for growing into them and there is a whole global family of sisters and brothers who are already shining like stars in all of the dark places longing for the light of a new day. Kelsey joins us all.

Another member brought a simple, ordinary receiving blanket. She had stitched it with the date and these words:

Kelsey Eric
Baptized into Christ
and
wrapped in his love forever

We wrapped Kelsey in his ordinary, holy receiving blanket and introduced him to his new siblings in Christ in this congregation. We told him he would never need any other security blanket! This one was for hanging onto every day. This one was to be a reminder of the comfort of God's love everyday, everywhere, no matter what.

New Relationships

Certificates were given as reminders to pray and talk together about this new relationship with God and God's people. I gave a copy of the catechism we use to the parents. I asked them to do an odd thing: to read the section on baptism aloud to Kelsey while rocking him or tucking him into bed. This is for a bonding in faith that goes beyond the words.

A young child in the congregation presented a seashell to everyone as they walked past the font on their way to the Lord's Table to be fed on the promises of Christ. I encouraged all of them to put water in the shell and use it daily in marking themselves with the sign of the Cross, the sign of our baptismal life in Christ.

Following worship, the congregation had another party, a celebratory meal together. Somehow, in the fast-paced world of high mobility for these young professional people, we were privileged to offer an oasis of God's grace. Glad and grateful, we shared our ordinary expressions of love and said good-bye.

Later that week, as we gathered around our family-talk council table, we spoke of how much this baptism had meant to all of us. But mostly we talked of how we would continue to support this family. I telephoned the pastors of the four congregations and asked them to be invitational. These were not mere "I'm passing a name on to you" calls. I shared passionately our congregation's concern for a place of worship, learning, fellowship, and service for this family. Six-year-old Matt had been all ears, eyes, and questions following his brother's baptism. His parents had used the occasion to retell him of his baptism. These pastors heard our special concern of not losing the momentum of openness at this time.

The council members wanted to write the family on a monthly basis. "I'll write this week," and "I'll send a note the first of next month" is the way they eagerly committed themselves. We received a warm card of thanks from Jodi and Jon shortly after the baptism Sunday. They had been deeply moved by all of the ordinary expressions of love they had received from the members.

But as the weeks followed into months we heard nothing from them. From time to time I tried to reach them by telephone, but no one ever answered. We waited and wondered. We inquired of Betty and Mabel. Nobody seemed to be hearing from them.

Fifteen months later, in mid-June of the following year, I dialed the home in Pennsylvania. "Hello!" It was Jodi. Immediately we picked up where we had left off. Twenty-month-old Kelsey was growing. "We'll send you pictures," she promised. Yes, they had found their way to one of the congregations. It was a new mission start. Occasionally they visited an older established church. "And I must tell you," Jodi exclaimed, "Kelsey uses his blanket every day! And we're coming to visit Grandma and Grandpa later this summer. We'll be in church with you. We can hardly wait! And our other good news," she continued, "is that we are moving back to Chicago in three and a half weeks. We'll be near my mother. And her church is right next door. We hope to make that our church home." All of this tumbled out of Jodi, reflecting a longing for home of more than one kind.

Next month we will talk some more at our family council time. Ordinary ministry of those baptismally clothed in Christ is ongoing. God keeps on with us! We wonder. We hope. We act. We forget. We receive. We give. We wait. We pray. All the while, God's Spirit is at work making of us once again a new creation in Christ.

CHAPTER EIGHT

Ordinary Courage: The Ministry of Justice

Mary A. Rowland

Mary, where are you going? Outside the gates? Inside the walls to a place where public policy dictates the lives of ordinary citizens? Where does one find faith communities in the midst of societal struggle? Mary's ministry raises questions for every context concerning judgment, responsibility, opportunity, and community. Where does our call to liberating ministry lead? And how does one sustain one's courage for prophetic, justice-seeking care?

Spring

On the way to prison I prayed for Tyrone and Todd. The prison is miles away from the central city where our parish is, so I had ample time for prayer. I prayed for their families, for the prison staff, for our parish; and I prayed for my own direction in the visits to come.

Tyrone I knew well, the son of faithful congregational members who are also good neighbors to my family. Tyrone actually introduced his family to Reformation Church when he was a young boy. Reformation is a beautifully mixed congregation (by race, economics, age, and gender) in the heart of Milwaukee and at the heart of a neighborhood—specifically Tyrone's neighborhood.

Todd I had never met. His mother and sister were new members of our congregation and had asked if I would visit Todd.

I was on my way to prison on my day off. That was because another parish member in prison had asked me to pick up his personal belongings to take to his wife, and this was the only day of the week one was allowed to receive such property.

When I arrived, dressed in my clergy shirt to make entrance supposedly easier, I proceeded through the gates and industrial-strength doors that securely slammed behind me. A guard informed me that the prisoner whose property I wanted to pick up had been transferred to a "more secure" facility (which is a six- to eight-hour bus ride away from the city where his family lives).

While waiting for the guard's computer to locate my other parishioners, I chatted with my next-door neighbor, Laura, who teaches a variety of classes at the prison, from English to welding. Like her, many persons who live in the city have chosen vocations that impact urban realities. Laura's presence lifts me as her neighbor, and her presence that day lifted me as a fellow minister among God's people who are in prison.

The guard directed me to a "less secure" work camp at the bottom of the hill to see both Tyrone and Todd. I was grateful when I realized I would not have to visit with them through glass and a telephone receiver.

Unexpectedly, the guards behind the desk asked me about my being a pastor, what "kind" of pastor I was, and who allows women to be priests. The question they asked with some hesitation was why a pastor, let alone a woman pastor, would come all that way just to see some guys who had broken the law. "God has claimed us all," I said. "Now is one time I really need to proclaim that to them."

The guard first brought Tyrone. I automatically hugged Tyrone as he entered and we sat at a table in a room that could have been a small cafeteria. No one else was present. He said that I was the first person he had touched in four months. Tyrone went on to tell me about his case, and how much longer he had to wait for his hearing. Possession of a gun had gotten him into this situation.

Weapons are so prevalent in our city that they are easy to come by. So guns are often handy when anger flares, and it can suddenly lead to a violent shooting. Tyrone had himself been injured by a gunshot the year before. In his present case the police had found the illegal weapon before anyone was hurt.

Before our time was up, Tyrone asked me if I would give his mom some flowers and a card with his name on it for Mother's Day. We shared the Lord's Supper and parted after holding hands in prayer.

When Todd was ushered into the same room, my physical contact with him was a hearty handshake, no less appreciated by him. I explained my presence and he proceeded to tell me his story. He had been arrested for violence against his girlfriend. Part of his work in prison was to attend an anger management group. I encouraged him to continue with this when he was released. I let him know that the Reformation parish had a fine relationship with such a group. Following his sharing I read Psalm 103, and we prayed together. He was then called to return to his work.

This was merely one segment of one day of one minister in the parish where Reformation Church is rooted. And in such ministry grace abounds! My colleague, Mick Roschke, calls it "grace for the moment."

There is grace when human beings who have been deprived of touch come back "in touch." There is grace when a pastor "out-of-touch" meets honesty in the eyes and words of community men. There is grace when mothers receive an extension of their sons through flowers. (Neither mom was able to visit her son often due to distance, lack of transportation, and other family attentions.)

Spring, One Year Later

A year later I found myself sitting behind a microphone at a subcommittee meeting of the Milwaukee County Board of Supervisors. That caused my heart to race and my face to flush much like prison gates and doors slamming behind me did. I was called to be in both places.

The issue at the county meeting was about treatment for persons who have alcohol and other drug addictions (AODA) and do not have insurance. In a move to cut costs the county administration "froze" all possibility for persons to receive county-paid treatment until the books were balanced. The administration made this move because all the budgeted funds for AODA treatment had been used up by April. As I said in a letter to the county administrator, "Once again the poor pay for the mistakes of the rest of us."

Knowing this is often true, the faith-based power organization, MICAH (Milwaukee Inner-city Congregations Allied for Hope) has been the critic and conscience of our county concerning AODA issues for years. A few years ago the county budget included $14 million for AODA treatment for persons without insurance. The amount dropped steadily until three years later when MICAH shouted, "STOP!" as I joined twenty-five ecumenical church leaders in an overnight "pray-in" in the county administrator's office.

> *A commonly held attitude is that crime should be punished rather than that a person be restored.*

After repeated, and repeatedly ignored, requests for a meeting with the County Executive, we went to his office with the plan that we would stay until he met with us *and* met our demands. He did meet with us, but did not respond. So we stayed in his office all night. Sheriff's deputies stayed with us and allowed us out of the office only to use the bathroom, and even then, under escort.

Using a cellular phone, we kept in contact with our lead organizer and one county supervisor who shares our passion on this issue. With their work outside and our prayers inside, there was a quorum of the County Board on Supervisors by 8:00 o'clock the next morning. Members of the press had stayed until after midnight the night before and returned very early that morning. All of this led to a promised minimum budget amount for the next few years for AODA referral and treatment.

The Springs to Come

The struggle continues. Today, during the writing of this chapter, MICAH confronted the whole County Board of Supervisors again! It seems that it is too easy for county to blame state, and state to blame county or federal funding sources for the shortage of funds.

Two underlying attitudes make our work very difficult. One is that many people consider drug addictions a moral affair, rather than a health/medical affair. A second commonly held attitude is that crime should be punished, rather than that a person be restored. Our state governor promoted biases when he rejoiced in the now fully implemented welfare reform, leaving thousands of persons with no insurance and no income, which in turn leads to more drugs and more crime. (Now in Wisconsin, 80 percent of persons in prison are there due to crimes related to drugs—either selling or using or some other crime committed while high or feeding the habit.) But the governor also encourages our state to build more prisons, and provide for AODA treatment programs in those prisons.

Thus our leaders leave us in a double bind. So our only hope is in Christ, who calls us to provide more opportunities for persons to get well *before* prison becomes the answer.[1] So how do I connect that ordinary day on the way to prison and this ordinary day in the county offices? And what do those days have to do with ministry in a nurturing community? Our faith community persistently hears Isaiah's "if you offer your food to the hungry and satisfy the needs of the afflicted . . . you shall be called the repairer of the breach, the restorer of streets to live in" (Isaiah 58:10 and 12*b*).

This community—ordinary human beings grounded in Word and sacrament ministry—nurtures Tyrone. This community is where Tyrone now finds himself most Sundays and many other times during a week. This is where he guides our youngsters back into worship after the extended sharing of Christ's peace. This is where he gracefully holds his toddling nephew while both receive Christ in the meal of life. This is where Tyrone receives and lives grace.

This ordinary community of faith, empowered by studying the Word and sharing the meal, visits those in prison (Matthew 25:36) and spends its life on behalf of the oppressed (Isaiah 58). Extraordinary grace *abounds* in a life for justice and extraordinary grace *calls* our communities into a life for justice.

Note

1. See Howard Zehr in *Changing Lenses: A New Focus for Crime and Justice* (Scottsdale, Pa.: Herald Press), 1990. Zehr makes the case that prison is too quickly seen as an answer to society's problems.

CHAPTER NINE

Ordinary Time: Intergenerational Ministry

Karen Rask Behling and Carol J. Rask

The Gospel winds its way through history by one generation telling the stories to the next. A daughter and mother coauthor this chapter (Carol's words are in italics). How do we build in time to tell the good news of God through telling the stories of God's faithful people? And what do we do when the previous generation no longer lives down the road? How can the faith community liberate Christians to put into words the hope that lies within them, telling the story to those who have not yet heard?

We gathered with Marvin and his family at the hospital. Marvin was dying. The cancer that had been managed was now assuming control; the end of the battle seemed imminent. We took our turns, going in a few at a time, to be with Marvin and his wife, Elaine. When I as pastor entered, I was joined by Marvin's son, Jim, along with the newest grandchild, three-month-old Matthew.

I read from Scripture—I don't recall what passage it was. I prayed with the family—I don't remember my words. And then Jim spoke. His words, I remember. Before he spoke, he came in close to his dying father. He leaned down, holding Matthew so that Grandpa could reach out to caress that tiny hand. "I'm going to tell him all about you, Dad," Jim said. "He's going to know all about you. And all of those stories that you told me about your dad. All those stories that you told me while we were mending fence; I'm going to tell him just like you told me." We stood in silence as Jim choked out his words, tears streaming down each person's face.

Marvin's life of faith would be remembered and retold. In telling his son, Matthew, the stories about Grandpa and Great-grandpa before him, Jim would be teaching his son what it means to live in faithfulness to God. To speak of Marvin was to speak of a man who had spent his life working the land and caring for the land—God's land. To speak of Marvin was to speak also of the God in whom he placed his trust. To speak of Marvin was to proclaim God's faithfulness to the next generation.

A Sacred Place

My family and I are reminded of the generations who have gone before us every time we look out our kitchen window. We live right next to a cemetery. As pastor, I appreciate being able to walk with the bereaved right from the funeral service to the graveside, but I hadn't realized what a blessing the cemetery would be to my children and our family. We go for walks in the cemetery, and look for the various symbols carved into stone--the crosses, the lilies, the lambs marking where the babies lie. We read the names, nearly all of whom we have never met. We have come to know at least some of them through the stories that others tell. We see the stones carved for those who are not yet dead, but who have chosen their final resting spot beside loved ones.

The cemetery has become for my family a wonderful sacred space, and our time walking there has become sacred time. It is our time to talk, our time to tell stories, our time to deal with the most basic questions of every child: Who am I? Where did I come from? Where am I going? So many of the gravestones are wonderful testimonies of faith; a few carefully chosen words or a symbol expresses trust and hope in God. Who are all of these buried in this cemetery? Each one is a child of God. That was true when they lived on this earth. That continues to be true after they die and are returned to the earth.

A Cloud of Witnesses

My children know of Adam and Eve whom God created from the earth. They know well the stories of Noah and Jonah; they use their dolls and toys to reenact the Christmas and Easter stories. They know of the faithfulness of Abraham and Sarah, and through our conversations in the cemetery, they are coming to know more about the faithfulness of people from the more recent past. To use the language of Hebrews 12, their "cloud of witnesses" is expanding as we learn about those who rest in the cemetery.

As I was growing up in the 1940s and 1950s, some of the people who made up my "cloud of witnesses" gathered every Sunday afternoon at Grandma and Grandpa's house. The Sabbath was a day of rest, not just for our family, but for all of the others on neighboring farms as well. Certainly the men fed the livestock and milked the cows, but that was about it. Dad never considered doing fieldwork on Sunday. Inside, we spent our Saturdays getting ready for Sunday by cleaning house and preparing food for the next day. The idea was to put Sunday dinner on the table as quickly and effortlessly as possible.

Sunday afternoons were spent gathered with relatives at Grandma and Grandpa's house. We were expected to be there. Though we weren't there for a full dinner, our afternoon "lunch" always began and ended with prayer. We kids wouldn't dare leave the table until the final thanksgiving prayer was offered.

Back then we didn't have many choices for recreational activities. Church was really the only game in town—especially in our rural neighborhood. Church was where we worshiped, learned, worked, and served together. I knew most everybody, and certainly everybody knew me and to which family I belonged. At times while I was growing up, that seemed to have its disadvantages; word of some misbehavior always seemed to make it home. But it was also significant to be known. I knew that I belonged in that community of believers; I knew that my life mattered to others.

After I grew up and married, my family didn't live down the road. When I was raising my children, Karen and Tim, we did have a wonderful baby-sitter, a woman from the congregation who became a surrogate grandmother to our children. If I was doing a service project she wouldn't take money; she said, "I can't do those things at church, but I can take care of your children."

My nine-year-old daughter is attending school in her third community. We have moved from state to state; Grandma and Grandpa don't live down the road. I remember when I grew up there were just four of us in our family, so my parents would invite others to our holiday tables. From the first months of our marriage, my husband and I have taken to doing the

We teach through stories so that others might be rooted in the faith.

same. When we moved to our new home out in the country, my third parish call, we began once again the process of meeting many new people, learning their names and faces.

One of those people was Bill. He was a grandpa who liked kids. He came early to church to fold the bulletins, and he stayed late visiting with his many friends of all ages. Less than three months after we moved here, Bill died suddenly of a heart attack. We had lost our friend. When grave diggers came early one morning, my four-year-old and his younger sister wanted to watch. After their older sister came home on the school bus, they showed her where Bill would be buried. Someone they knew would now be buried in the midst of this cemetery. It became a daily pilgrimage. I don't know if Bill's family ever wondered where all of the dandelion bouquets came from, but it became important to my children to remember Bill in this way.

Our children had known Bill, but much more important, Bill had known them. He had known their names. Bill had loved God. Bill had loved them, and they in turn, had loved Bill. Bill continues to play a significant role in their lives of faith as he joins that great "cloud of witnesses." Bill's life and death along with our walks in the cemetery make the message of Easter concrete for them. This is where the hope in Christ's resurrection meets our everyday lives.

Knowing You Are Part of God's Family

That's the gift that Jim received from his father, Marvin, and is passing on to his son; the gift of being led into the future strengthened by the stories of God's people from the past. We teach through stories so that others might be rooted and built up and established in the faith. For Jim, this meant having his father share stories while they mended fence. Marvin had given Jim the gift of turning a rather ordinary task into sacred time, to lead his son in understanding who he was; Jim was not just a member of their family but also God's family. That would make a difference in how he lived his life, now and in his future.

As I was growing up, I recall opportunities that my parents claimed as sacred time and space. There were daily family meals that began with prayer and included conversations about the day, and ended, at least during the season of Advent, with family devotions. We gathered around the Advent wreath in the living room, our only light coming from the candles as we anticipated the birth of the one sent by God to be the Light of the World. I remember Sunday mornings that included not just worship and Sunday school, but also going as a family to deliver meals to the elderly. That powerful combination of worshiping and learning was put into practice. As a teenager, I also experienced sacred time after school at the kitchen table talking to Mom not only about my day at school, but also about what she was learning in her classes at seminary.

I remember sitting at the kitchen table with Karen. It was just ordinary time. Sometimes she asked "Mother, why aren't you like other mothers who decorate cakes and sew my clothes?"

When I was younger I had begged mother to sew me an outfit and she did (I must have been in the third or fourth grade). But I never asked her again because I saw how much work it was for her to do something that was not her gift. So I learned to sew.

Karen saw me minister as volunteer in the community, in the local congregation, and on regional boards and committees; and, she heard about my classes at seminary. I don't think at that time she had thought much about what she was going to do after high school. But the story was told. The children heard stories I didn't know I was telling.

Keep the Word; Share the Story!

Life on the farm offered my parents many opportunities to connect faith with our daily living. How we cared for the land and the animals and were careful not to waste resources connected our faith with God's charge to be responsible stewards. God also had entrusted to my parents the raising of children, a responsibility they took most seriously. By virtue of our rural situation, my parents had to be our primary teachers of the faith. Our church was able to offer services only twice per month, and one of those was conducted in Norwegian. Since my German mother and we children didn't speak Norwegian, we stayed home those Sundays and held our own worship service and Bible lessons. By the time we started Sunday school in first grade, my parents already had taught us many Bible stories. We didn't wait until confirmation to begin memorizing songs, Bible verses, and catechism. My parents would work with us, until the words flowed out of our mouths as naturally as breathing.

> Hear, O Israel: The LORD is our God, the LORD alone. You shall love the LORD your God with all your heart, and with all your soul, and with all your might. Keep these words that I am commanding you today in your heart. Recite them to your children and talk about them when you are at home and when you are away, when you lie down and when you rise. (Deuteronomy 6:4-7)

We have stories to tell our children: old, old stories of Jesus and his love; stories from the Bible and stories from our own lives. We need to claim the moments to share those stories; regular, intentional moments that can become sacred times. When we are at home and when we are away, we can claim time with our families, with our sisters and brothers in Christ. When we rise in the morning, when we go to bed at night, when we eat together, when we work together, when we walk together, and play together, we can claim the time as story time—faith story time.

77

We as faith communities face a new challenge today. Young parents need other nurturing adults in their lives. My daughter, as a pastor, and her husband, need such caring people in their lives. Some places you find them, and some places you don't. We live in an era when we pay people for everything in our lives. We need to learn again how to care for each other.

Creating New Opportunities

I've experienced an incredible number of deaths in the past month— seven in all, including a friend and colleague on the local library board, an aunt, and finally my father in December. Since my mother's death, he played the central role of connecting our family. I knew that most of his friends had already died or would be physically unable to come to the funeral. But when we drove home, I was surprised to find so many people had come not only to the funeral—two days before Christmas—but also served a dinner for all of us. It was the children of my father's generation who provided support now because my father had been seen as a central caring person in that community for years. Two-year-old Emma, my father's great-granddaughter, wondered why he would not be buried in "their cemetery" next to the parsonage where she walked and played each day.

How do we minister across generations in larger congregations? In urban areas? When there are so many alternative ways for people to spend their time? How can we reshape in a new way this caring community? People need to know each other, to suffer and rejoice with one another and in so doing tell and live the story of Jesus Christ in their lives.

In preparation for All Saints' Day we invited people to write things they remembered about life in the congregation on a time line posted in the narthex. They were hesitant at first, assuming their personal memories were insignificant. People just don't tell their stories automatically; but gradually, people felt free to add their words. Someone remembered the day of a baptism when the heat went out, so it was held at home. Over the next two weeks our composite story began to appear. On All Saints' Sunday after worship, we held a potluck meal and then walked through the time line together, as we encouraged one another to tell stories so others could hear them. Most people have lived here their whole lives, but we all heard new stories that day and gained a deeper appreciation of our roots here in this community of faith.

During each Wednesday of Lent this year, we had a supper along with a brief time of worship and a Bible study entitled "Wilderness Wanderings." In studying Abraham and Sarah, we made connections with ancestors who left homelands in response to God, and with our own life's journeys as well. Abraham's sacrifice of Isaac challenged us to name sacrifices we and others have made. Jacob and Esau's rivalry and eventual reconciliation invited us to name and remember relationships made whole again.

The week before Memorial Day people come out to the cemetery to plant flowers. Every evening I make it a point to be there and ask questions. I had noticed that one child had died just days shy of his fourth birthday. I talked with his parents. They said, "Of course you know. . . ." But I didn't, so I asked, and in the retelling they remembered precious times as well as the grief. Another member always takes care of the "baby" row in the cemetery. She doesn't know all the babies, but she plants flowers anyway, every year, together with her daughter and her granddaughter and her great-granddaughter, and my daughter who joins in this gift of remembrance.

Such intergenerational ministry can happen so simply, but oftentimes it takes intentional effort to make those connections and encourage the sharing of stories:

- Plan activities with others, whether on a household, neighborhood, or congregational level; take the initiative to bring people together.
- Invite people to spend holidays with you; encourage others to do so too.
- Ask people to talk about their work, their heritage, their traditions, their hobbies. "I'd really like to know about. . . ." We're never too old for "show-and-tell"; go to their home or workplace, listen and learn.
- Lift up people's talents, gifts, and expertise so that they will tell their stories. Ask questions and name as significant what they assume is "unimportant" or "ordinary."

We all have stories. It's a matter of being intentional about sharing them. It's a matter not of finding the time, but claiming the time, making the time, naming the time as God's time to share the liberating Word of God at work in the world.

CHAPTER TEN

Ordinary Concern: The Ministry of Companionship

April Ulring Larson

Two church bodies. Two bishops. Twin daughters. Companions! Christ becomes a word of comfort between traveling companions. Do we who preach in public know how to put the gospel into words for our friends? From halfway around the world, from one who has known the depths of danger, Bishop April, her family, and the churches she serves hear the power of the gospel. When we meet each other on the road, and say, "How are you?" do we really listen to the answer?

This past summer our synod was gifted with the presence of our companion synod bishop, the Rev. Wakseyoum Idossa. President Wakseyoum learned as a very young leader of the Ethiopian Evangelical Church Mekane Yesus what it means to suffer for the sake of Jesus Christ. Along with many other church leaders—some of whom were killed, others imprisoned and tortured—Wakseyoum Idossa experienced the cost of following Jesus during the dangerous days of the seventeen-year national communist rule.

This same church that suffered so grievously under the totalitarian communist regime now is the fastest growing Lutheran church in the world.

It was the great honor and privilege of our synod to host President Wakseyoum. Together he and I visited almost every parish in our synod. President Wakseyoum was also a keynote speaker for our church body's annual National Global Mission Events, one of which was held in our own city, hosting over two thousand people at our local university campus.

An Evening of Crisis

On Saturday evening of that global mission event my husband, Judd, and I returned home about 10:30 and were very surprised to see the living room in chaos. Our Bible-camp-counselor daughters' clean clothes were still lying in piles waiting to be packed. Our daughters had attended a wedding in Iowa and should have been home, packed, and departed hours ago to return to camp. I knew something was wrong. It had already been an evening of crisis. The coordinating chair of the Global Mission Event, who was also my assistant, had ended up in the hospital emergency room, and our office manager's father-in-law, who lived with them, was suddenly ill and fighting for his life in another hospital. As judicatory staff, the fragility of life was clearly and suddenly pressing upon all of us.

While our twin daughters were traveling to the wedding reception, they became lost on one of the treacherous northeast Iowa gravel roads. I grew up in that area and I know how deadly the twists and turns can be. Most of us who grew up there had lost classmates on those roads. Katie had not seen a sharp turn and drop in the road until it was too late. She reacted incorrectly by braking and the car went out of control, quickly gaining speed down the steep hill. The car hit the ravine, rolled over and slid upside down for about a hundred yards. Our daughters, hanging upside down by their seat belts, escaped uninjured through a window, although the station wagon was totaled.

Strangely enough, the automobile accident happened quite close to my brother's home. An older couple who witnessed the accident came to our daughters' assistance and brought them to my brother's house. My father, who had been delayed traveling across Iowa to attend the Global Mission Event, had stopped by my brother's house to say hello. While there the twins arrived. It was my father who then drove our frightened but uninjured daughters back to our home in Wisconsin.

Even though I was so deeply thankful for our daughters' safety, I was still shaken by their accident. Parents struggle with the fear of losing one or more of their children in an accident. Since our twins are so often together, I had often worried that we could lose them both at once.

Words of Powerful Concern and Witness

What a peculiar course of events. But what I remember more than anything was the reaction of our dear friend and brother in Christ, President

Wakseyoum, to the news of our daughters' accident. As Americans, if every-thing turns out okay, that ends the discussion. I know that. We are con-cerned for one another, but if a potential tragedy has a good outcome, there is no need to talk any longer. President Wakseyoum's reac-tion stood out in stark con-trast to anyone else's.

> *He fixed his eyes on me and his eyes would not let me go.*

When he heard on Sunday from others what had happened to our daughters, this man of restraint in speech and elegant manners, who walked with such grace and ease, ran across the university campus to find us. When he found us, he asked me, "What happened?" Actually, I can't remember what he asked, all I know is he didn't let me drop the subject. He fixed his eyes on me and his eyes would not let go. He kept questioning me to find out *all* that had happened. I *knew* he was very concerned and that he was not afraid to show it. Through his eyes and the expression on his face, he commu-nicated his intense presence with me. It was very clear that right now this topic of discussion was more important to him than anything else. I was almost embarrassed. After all, the girls were fine. But, oh how I needed to talk about it!

His ministry to me and to my husband did not end there. He was stay-ing at our house. When it was time to pray together and then retire to bed, President Waukesyoum said to our son, "Ben, go get the Bible." Our son brought a Bible and Wakseyoum read the first three verses of Psalm 126:

> When the LORD restored the fortunes of Zion,
>   we were like those who dream.
>   Then our mouth was filled with laughter,
>   and our tongue with shouts of joy;
>   then it was said among the nations,
> "The LORD has done great things for them."
> The LORD has done great things for us,
>   and we rejoiced.

Then he put down the Bible, once again locking his eyes on ours. This great leader who often spoke in a voice so quiet I could barely hear, spoke with passion and with power and with a conviction I have seldom experi-enced in my life: "The Global Mission Event was filled with the power of the Holy Spirit, every part, every speaker, the whole event." Then he said words very unfamiliar to my theological training but words I still remem-ber. "The event was filled with the Holy Spirit. The devil wants to take away the joy of the people by attacking the leaders and their families. Katie and Amy's lives will never be the same. They have been given back their lives and from now on, every day belongs to God."

I do not know how to assess these words of President Wakseyoum, who has walked as a young leader with his church through enormous suffering. He walked through threats to his family and the threat of death to himself. I do not know how to assess his words, but this I know: This bishop of the fastest growing Lutheran Church in the world, who lived for seventeen years in constant threat and daily danger, knows intimately that we do not fight with flesh and blood, but with principalities and powers.

I also know that this dear brother in Christ proclaimed Jesus Christ to us in an hour of deepest need when we would not and could not ask for it. He was a companion to us when the fragility of life came so very near. He was our pastor. He spoke out loud the living word of Jesus Christ. He didn't just walk alongside us but actually spoke a word that burned in our fearful hearts and carried the healing power of Christ into our aching bodies.

In the six weeks he was with us, President Wakseyoum visited every parish in our synod. Everywhere he challenged us to imagine a God who calls the church to love the whole person and the whole community. His church has four parts to its mission: proclamation, education, development, and health care. The Ethiopian Evangelical Church Mekane Yesus (which means "dwelling of God") believes Christ calls us to care for the whole person and the whole community. They do not separate deed from word, or speaking from action. It is all connected. Nor do they separate the individual from his or her community.

In our culture we often say, "How are you?" as an ordinary word of concern, not really expecting an answer, or not really listening to it when one is given. When someone presents us with a significant need, we may care desperately but we often become debilitated and don't know how to respond. We may even become embarrassed, believing our words may appear nosy or seem to imply they can't take care of themselves. People think pastors know the right words to say, but I struggle with putting the gospel into words for my friends. I find myself hungering to be around sisters and brothers in Christ from the two-thirds world. I need to experience their theology of God and of the church.

A Need to Learn from Our Companions

I long to understand the words of my first close global friend, Rachel Maulaga from Tanzania, the executive director of the women in her diocese. I once asked, "Rachel, how long does it take you to walk to work?"

"Well, if I go the direct way it takes a half hour, but if I go around the back way it takes just a few minutes."

"What do you mean, Rachel? Why does the direct, main way take longer?"

"Because," she answered, "with each person I must say, `How are you? How are your children? How is your husband or wife? How is your work? and listen to their answers."

Rachel used to make fun of how long Americans talk on the phone, particularly on long-distance calls. She thought it was wasteful and extravagant. When she called her bishop to tell him when she would return to Tanzania, I asked her, both teasing slightly and testing her commitment to concern for relationships, "Rachel, you were in a hurry. Did you ask your bishop sentence by sentence, 'How are you? How is your wife? How is your work? How are the children?' "

Her answer, given her strong concern about extravagant phone calls, surprised me: "Of course!" She could not cut it short. (The bishop had given brief responses to her full complement of questions—financial considerations, of course, were a consideration.) To just say, "How are you?" without expecting a real response would not do, because relationship is always more important than task or time.

Then I said, "You have been away from your children for nine months. How long will it take you to get from Dar es Salaam to home?"

She said, "Well, if I go by bus, it will take many days because I must stop and see my sister and other relatives along the way, but if I get a ride from the Swedish missionary, I can travel directly to my children."

"Won't you be in trouble with your sister?"

"No, if I'm riding with the missionary my sister knows I can't stop to visit her."

A wonderful irony! Rachel, who was so eager to see her children, could take advantage not only of the ride but of what might be considered rude practices of Europeans and Americans, to set aside the protocol of her own culture on this one occasion.

Community, companionship, relationships are to Rachel and Wakseyoum more important than the clock and accomplishing tasks. President Wakseyoum, a visitor in a culture that says, "If no one is seriously hurt, we move on," brought Judd and me back to the place where we truly were and ministered to us with the invasive power of God's word and presence.

CHAPTER ELEVEN

Ordinary Letter: The Ministry of Preaching

Virginia Anderson-Larson

Ginger uses words purposefully, like the careful lead pastor she is. Her thoughtful response to a letter moves her to a sermon and from a sermon to education. Where do the words begin and where do they culminate? Preaching is a communal vocation of proclamation, breaking open the Word, which people then carry into the public world.

In the first week in Lent, as my husband and I ate a late, leisurely breakfast on a Friday morning in March, he motioned toward the letter from Stephanie that was lying on the kitchen counter. "Quite a letter!" he said. "Yes it is," I sighed. "There's almost a sermon in responding to it."

Then it dawned on me what I had said; the as yet unwritten sermon for Sunday broke loose in my mind. The assigned text for the upcoming Sunday was Jesus' mother hen description of his love for Jerusalem. It was a text that, in sixteen years of preaching, I had not yet preached upon. In my excitement to finally have the opportunity to preach from this text, I must have shut down all my creative processes. I had come home late Thursday night with still no sermon title or focus for preaching. Even after having done my preparatory reading, studying of Scripture, and perusing of several books with preaching helps, I was sermonless!

This first week of Lent had been long and full, including a midweek Lenten sermon and the funeral of Russ, a faith-filled member of the congregation who died after an extended illness. In my tiredness that Thursday evening, I had quickly read the letter from my niece, Stephanie, and then laid it back down on the kitchen counter. She was asking me what it meant to be a godmother, because a friend had asked her to serve in this role. I knew I needed to write back to Stephanie, but it would take some time to prepare a thoughtful response. In the beginning of this Lenten season I could foresee no such opportunity until after Easter. I placed the letter on the counter, however, as a visual reminder that I wanted to attend to it.

I now reached for the letter. As I reread it, I found myself imagining that I was reading the letter to the congregation on Sunday. The congregation just might hear their own questions as I read Stephanie's letter to them. It described her friend's situation as an unmarried, unchurched high school student who was asking her best friend to be godmother for her baby.

The preparatory studying and reading done earlier in the week found its voice in the response to Stephanie's question. In the gospel Jesus spoke of loving as a mother. The text provided rich, poignant ways to talk about how God's protective, caring, forgiving love is offered to us, if only we will receive it; if only we will be gathered under God's wings of love. The role of a godmother included teaching and modeling this for a child who was to grow up in the faith. The Spirit seemed to be weaving this beautiful teaching of God's love into a real-life situation through a response to Stephanie's question.

From Letter to Text to Sermon

My day off is not a sermon-writing day. Today, however, was different. I headed for my favorite chair in the living room, picked up my journal and wrote as fast as I could write. This was exciting! The gospel metaphor stirred memories from my childhood years of a chicken coop and the protective cackling of the hens when we went to gather eggs. I remembered Stephanie's own baptism, when the pastor instructed her sponsors to "get snoopy" into her parents' lives if they fell lax in the promises they made, promises to teach her the faith, bring her to worship and learning times in their community of faith, and be examples of faithful Christian living.

That journal entry became the basis for the sermon when I returned to my study on Saturday morning. After editing and fine-tuning the way in which the gospel's gentle, caring love spoke to this particular situation, the sermon took shape in two parts: the reading of Stephanie's letter and my response to Stephanie's question.

Many of the congregation were deeply moved as they heard the sermon on that weekend. The rather intimate style in which the gospel was proclaimed captured their interest. This real-life scenario was familiar in their family and circles of friends. To mother like God had taken on meaning for them. A familiar text had come to life through Stephanie's letter and provided a new meaning for them and their relationships: to mother like God.

In retrospect it became clearer for me how God was providing abundantly in this deeply meaningful, but incredibly demanding Lenten season. Stephanie's letter was initially one more request of time that it seemed I didn't have to give. Yet, under the Holy Spirit's creative power, that which I could easily have overlooked was the impetus to dig deeply into the biblical text, to relate it to contemporary questions from young adults, and to offer life-related connections.

From Funeral Sermon to Learning Opportunity

In retrospect, it also seemed like an eternity since Russ's funeral. In reality, his funeral had happened only two days before Stephanie's letter arrived. The week, however, had been long and full. The conversations after worship that following Sunday were filled with expressions of appreciation for the Sunday sermon that included Stephanie's letter, and for the sermon at Russ's funeral. By this time, it was five days since Russ's funeral. Why was it that people were still talking about that sermon?

As I listened to what people were saying, I heard that the funeral was so personal and so filled with promise and hope. They said it had reflected who Russ was.

Just a week earlier I had sat with Russ and his wife at the hospital, and planned the funeral service with them. The choices reflected what was important to Russ in his life and faith in God. Those at the funeral service recognized a difference in the tenor of the service. They now came to me asking for some kind of tool so that they might also attend to plans fitting their own situation and life.

It was the prompting and encouragement of several people that kept the project of creating such a planning tool on task. Pastoral life, in my experience, in the midst of the Lenten season does

> *People were asking for help in facing the reality of dying in the midst of their living.*

not usually allow time for creation of new, previously unplanned projects. However, in reflecting on the nature of the Lent/Easter season, my pastoral colleague, Tim, and I recognized a *kairos* moment. Our people were asking for help in facing the reality of dying in the midst of their living. What an invitation!

We chose to schedule a two-session adult forum. On Palm/Passion

Sunday, we introduced a three-page funeral planning form we had created. The dozen folks that were there eagerly received it. They were invited to complete it, and on the Sunday following Easter we would meet again to share stories and experiences from the process of completing the form.

My husband and I, at different times, had spoken of our desires for funeral and burial decisions, but had never written down our intentions. It was a timely moment for me to participate in the process I was encouraging the congregation to do. On the Monday evening of Holy Week I nestled into my favorite recliner. Surrounded by the quiet of my home, and in the presence of flickering candles, I began the process. Three hours later I emerged from what had been an incredible journey of sifting through scriptures, hymns, music, liturgy, significant relationships, and funeral practices that are important for me. I had not thought about dying—I had thought about living!

From Funeral Plans to Easter Sermon

Early the next morning, I received a phone call from my mother telling me about the fatal car accident of Phil, my brother-in-law's father. She reported that funeral plans were not yet made, and that they would take a while because the family had not made any prior funeral arrangements. Mother was hurting for my sister who lived halfway across the country. She needed to be making arrangements for traveling and being away from her young children to attend the funeral, but she could not make definite plans because the family could not decide when the funeral would be.

After listening to Mother's story, I sensed it was a gift moment for me to tell her my story of the previous evening. "Mom," I said, "I'm teaching an adult education class at church about funeral preplanning, and last night I filled out the form we are using in the class. I wrote down several of my desires for my funeral service some day, and among them are the burial of my ashes at Fremont" (the country cemetery of my childhood church).

"I don't know if they'll know how to bury ashes at Fremont," she said. "I don't think they've done that before."

"Well, Mom, now there's time to think about it," I suggested. We concluded our conversation soon thereafter, but in those moments, the sermon for Easter Sunday was already beginning to unfold. I asked myself the rhetorical question, "If there is ever a time when we ought to find the courage to face and deal with our own dying, is it not on Easter Sunday when the gospel of resurrection proclaims 'Christ is Risen'?"

I returned to Luke's Gospel. The angel's proclamation "He is risen" is not just a wonderful announcement. It is promise and hope that speaks to the dying each of us face. The sermon flowed as I wove the angel's proclamation into the reality of the myriad of feelings that thinking about one's own dying releases. This promise is for real. Easter is for each of us!

On the day of resurrection, in the midst of the majesty of the pipe organ ranks proclaiming "Jesus Christ is risen today," and the timpani and trumpets swelling the praise with their own reverberations of joy, each one in the pew was asked, during the sermon, to take out of their worship bulletin a funeral planning form.

"I hope you are not shocked to find it there," I spoke to those in the nearly full sanctuary, "for if resurrection offers anything to us, it offers us the courage and hope and freedom from fear to think about our own living, dying, and resurrection in a very practical way. This pertains to every person here. Not one of us is exempt from dying. Every one of us is offered the gift of eternal life *now* and into eternity. So I invite us to claim it now." I could feel the Spirit's power pulsing in me as I preached and sensed that the congregation was eagerly listening to what I was preaching.

I recalled the story of completing the funeral preplanning form myself earlier that week and then the ensuing telephone conversation with my mother. I invited the congregation into their own experience of such thought and preplanning as I continued to preach: "If the resurrection changes your reality at all, it offers you the freedom from fear to accept the reality that you will die. In that reality, trusting the promise of resurrection, you are free to give your family the gift of information and your personal wishes for your funeral that they will need to know at the time of your death. May your being in worship this morning be your invitation to the risen Jesus to change the reality of your life and fill you with all joy and peace in believing."

From Congregational Conversation to Public Proclamation

A week later, as we again gathered in the adult forum to share stories about using the funeral preplanning form, the hour was much too short. People reported: "We talked about funerals during our Easter dinner." "My husband still will not talk about anything that has to do with death." "Can I get another copy of the form for my mother?"

This became a *kairos* time in the congregation. Filling out the funeral preplanning form led to new questions. In response to the interest, we decided to include a copy of the form in the next edition of the congregation's newsletter. Among the readers of the newsletter was the religion editor for the city newspaper. She phoned me to say that she was intrigued with the form and wanted to write a feature article for the newspaper. Would I be willing to be interviewed?

The resulting article proclaimed to the entire metropolitan area the gift of funeral planning. On the front page, above the fold, the headline read "Funeral Planning: A Celebration of Life!" Within minutes after the church secretary arrived that morning, she received the first of many phone calls asking for a copy of the form. Those calls, and the requests from friends of congregational members, have continued ever since.

What a joy to reflect back over those weeks in Lent and Easter! What a privilege to see how ordinary life events, an illness leading to death and a letter from my niece, had become the contemporary means through which the scriptures might speak a life-giving word of Christ's resurrection to people two thousand years later. Russ and Stephanie did not know each other. They lived a half continent apart. Yet in the same week, they both touched my life. In and through their stories, the Holy Spirit found unimagined ways to weave the living Word of Jesus Christ into their stories and through their stories to enter the life story of those who heard the Word proclaimed. This is the promise and the hope of the biblical texts: those who come thirsting for living water and hungry for the bread of life are not disappointed. Thanks be to God.

CHAPTER TWELVE

Ordinary Journey: The Ministry of Visitation

Norma Cook Everist

There's nothing like making the rounds, whether at a St. Louis church potluck, or in an inner-city Detroit neighborhood. How do we do "walking-around" ministry? What are the theological questions raised during visitation? In desert and flood, city and open country, how does one help people reflect on the ministries in which they already are engaged?

"The visitor has come! The visitor has come!" Four-year-old Hannah had stayed up past her bedtime because she was excited. She had heard my car pull up outside her family's country home—actually an old schoolhouse converted to a parsonage.

I arrived late, not just by a four-year-old's schedule, but by mine. It was almost 8:00 P.M. I had been delayed leaving the seminary because of a crucial faculty meeting vote. But here I was, in the hidden valleys of rural Wisconsin, having turned off at County Road C. "Don't become confused and turn off at County Road CC . . . go beyond that," Tim had told me.

I was in the house only long enough to set down my suitcase and greet—and say good night to—the children when Tim, formerly a seminary student of mine and now a pastor, called from the church. He had just finished confirmation ministry class and asked if I was tired. "No? Well, then, I'll be home in five minutes and we'll go." Actually it took less than that because the church was just a cemetery away. We were off to a meeting of local citizens concerned about yet another failed school bond vote. I listened as people struggled with where to build a new consolidated school building to assure that each town's significance was retained. Two towns, seven years earlier, had decided they would "live" together. I reflected with Tim on the question of whether communities that had been joined for economic reasons, now, in the midst of conflict, could stay yoked. So many rural communities (schools *and* churches) face similar questions of identity, money, and mission.

After two days with Tim, including hospital visits and walking country roads, greeting neighbors and simply listening to Tim's solid, long-term commitment to rural ministry, I moved down the road just a few miles to spend time with Arnold in what, by contrast, seemed like a large town and a huge church. Here, too, I was quickly whisked off to his ministry in the community. We drove over to the local high school where Arnold had formed a partnership with the guidance counselor, working with youth. As "guest of the guest," Arnold introduced me to these students as his former teacher. He drafted me into an impromptu role play as we interacted with teens on issues of "commitment and marriage" in a family-living class.

During our days together, Arnold and I reflected on many issues of church, ministry, and community. How do churches work together appropriately with institutions and agencies in mutual concern for the youth of the community? What role do larger congregations play with smaller congregations in neighboring towns? Are they the self-sufficient "model"? Leader and teacher? Or also learners with and from rural congregations? Arnold and I were learning from each other as well.

Planning to Be Surprised

I was on sabbatical, observing through conversation—one could say "ethnographic research"—the congregations and ministries of our graduates who had been out of seminary one year, three years, and five years. I carefully had designed my approach: visit three men and three women—three married, three single—of various ages. Or one could say I just went to hang out with them for a few days.

Pastoral visitation is like that. You engage in a disciplined, yet relational way, planning the visits, but open to the surprises that come at each place. The issues and the questions actually arise from the conversation. My hosts wanted to prepare for my visit (I know of at least one pastor's study that got cleaned for the occasion, not unlike parishioners who generations ago may have made ready the parlor for the parson's visit). I also entered the clutter and confusion of ordinary daily lives.

Prom night dominated one household. Dinner table conversation swirled around the festivities and extended curfews. But still these P. K.s (pastor's kids) showed up at both services the next morning to lead children in song.

I came into the middle of their stories and left, wondering, where will Adam go to college? How did the new school bond issue turn out? When would the flood waters recede and what would be left of the farm? But I'm getting ahead of myself. . . .

> ### Read the books that are the people of God.

When I began this type of parish visitation ten years ago, driving ten thousand miles to visit thirty-seven congregations in all regions of this country over six months, I worried about my being an intrusion. My mother had taught me not to "bother people." But I soon discovered that my presence was welcome, and it helped pastors and parishioners theologically reflect on questions about their own journeys of faith. Visitation means listening, observing, reflecting. As a professor of church and ministry, I tell students they need to learn to think theologically inductively, as well as sytematically. They need to fully enter the context of their call and learn from people's lives. They need to read the books that are the people of God. I, also, need to keep on learning through visitation. The God who is on the journey with us, takes us on journeys with one another, creating all kinds of learning encounters.

John Wesley's words remind us not to make the parish our world, but to make the world our parish. I frequently fly to distant speaking engagements, but there's nothing like driving to a place if one wants perspective. One cannot appreciate Clovis, New Mexico, unless one has driven across that beautiful, vast, open—some would say empty—landscape. That's what I did a sabbatical ago.

Listening and Reflecting

The morning after I arrived in Clovis, we sat around a table in the church fellowship room eating a burrito breakfast (which included eggs, hash, fruit, and a box of doughnuts—just in case). This was the same table where we had gathered for Bible study the night before. I asked people why they had come to church here. They said in their pastor's hearing what they might not say directly to him: "It had been eighteen years since I was in church; spiritually I had left that church much before I actually left. I had given up trying to find a church. I'm not afraid to think and feel here." Another said, "I'm here today for the first time because I see the Spirit of God in my friend, Mel. This is the first place I've heard we are saved by grace and not by what we do." "Our pastor preaches about the importance of the Crucifixion and Resurrection. For people who have been bludgeoned by life changes, the church needs to be both an agent and an interpreter of change."

When I asked, "What difference does it make that the church is here?" people smiled knowingly among themselves. They told the visitor, "We move around a lot." No one present at that table had asked to come to Clovis, New Mexico. Most were sent on a tour of duty to the local military base; usually it had not been their first choice. "We know what an outsider feels like. Most of us come from someplace else." A woman confessed, "I took pictures of telephone poles going out into the distance and sent it to people to tell them what it's like here." This is a transient church, and it always will be.

Sitting on the Steps

Once pastoral visitation and theological reflection get into your bones, it seems hard to stop. So one day last summer, my husband, Burton, and I found ourselves sitting on the steps of Resureccion/Resurrection in the Hill section of New Haven, Connecticut, where Ruth has been a pastor for fifteen years. She had just seen off a busload of neighborhood children and youth on a day-long outing, but not before she had excitedly introduced me to Raynetta, the group's leader. Raynetta was the first from her family, and the first from this fledgling congregation, to graduate from college. A major focus of Resurrecion's mission is to help move youth out of the cycle of poverty and hopelessness by securing education. Ruth said, "In this neighborhood you can't buy milk after 8:00 at night, but you can buy drugs anytime."

The congregation, officially organized three years ago after many years as a mission church, struggles because most of its members are young and poor. How can a congregation be financially self-supporting if it is primarily full of youth? But such economic hardship is not the total reflection of Resurreccion. Because there are very few people in the congregation over forty, ministry, including leadership, is taken on by youth and young adults. The congregation now has fourteen people in college. And Raynetta? Well, she is in graduate school preparing to become a social worker with visions of coming right back to the Hill.

"I know most of the children around here," Ruth said, "but people who are poor are forced to move from neighborhood to neighborhood. You can get lost. And children grow and change. I had not seen one family of kids for some time and then one day, while driving back to the church, I caught a glimpse of kids who I thought might be them over on Clay Street, in another part of the city, coming out of a green house. So I went back and went to all the green houses on the block looking for them." Did she find them? Ruth, a wise shepherd in the city, never stops looking.

Making the Rounds

The current sabbatical rounds, to the "three men and three women" kept me closer to home, around the upper Midwest. I visited Donnita in Lost Nation; her two-point parish was actually just down the road a piece. I had driven Highway 151 many times on my way to Cedar Rapids or Des Moines. This day I turned off to find Lost Nation. Donnita was waiting for me, but we didn't stay long at the parsonage. She had pastoral rounds of her own to make, and I was invited along. This Saturday afternoon we drove to the supermarket in Maquoketa, to call on a team of parishioners taking their shift at the church-sponsored hot dog stand. "I didn't take a shift," she said. "This was their project and I knew they could carry it off. I planned to visit a number of shifts, supporting them in their community effort."

Oxford Junction (O.J.) and Lost Nation share a pastor. Donnita feels at home in this rural community, her second call, and wants to stay for awhile. She is single and has learned how to connect with other professional women through a book study group in a nearby larger community. Donnita recently became a mom to infant Megann Colleen XiuAn from China. She said, "Both congregations have supported me in this new role. In June we had a joint Sunday service in the community park so both churches could participate in Megann's baptism. She's part of this ministry now. One day when baby-sitting plans fell through, I took her to confirmation class. As I walked up and down the aisles among the youth, she followed in her walker. On one snowy winter night we held church council meeting at the parsonage. I sat on the floor with Megann, who was playing quietly with her toys. One can lead a meeting from the floor."

Keeping in touch with former students, such as Donnita, is a joy; however, one needs boundaries and role clarity, as in any pastoral relationship. And certainly, if I were a pastor serving a congregation I would not keep contact with former parishioners. My role in these visits is not pastor, not bishop, but, well, "visitor," carrying out a ministry of theological reflection through mutual learning. Because I have taught in divinity school and seminary settings for twenty-four years, I know I dare not become isolated from current congregational life, just as pastors need continuing education and theological reflection in their context.

Driving Through an Ocean

I had been scheduled the week following my visit with Tim and Arnold to drive to North Dakota and then back through Minnesota. At Arnold's home, before church on Sunday, we caught the news flash that not only was Grand Forks (North Dakota) totally flooded, but that fires now raced through the downtown. Floodwaters, following a winter of severe blizzards, were devastating large parts of western Minnesota, the Dakotas, and southern Manitoba. I called Steve, who served south of Fargo: "Should I come? Can I get through? Won't I be in the way of the emergency workers?" He responded, "No. You won't be in the way. I want you to come; I want you to experience this with us." We met in Fargo. After unloading a carload of food I had brought from people at our seminary at the ecumenically sponsored relief center, I followed Steve's car through what looked for all the world like the North Dakota Ocean. There was water as far as one could see, lapping at the sides of the interstate.

I spent three days observing ministry in the midst of great suffering. I saw that the floods that had overwhelmed the land had not yet overwhelmed the people. Their lives went on. They know that each year farming is a risk. When one might be driven to doubt God, the Protector, these faithful folk trusted a God whose covenant faithfulness was deep and steadfast. I watched as their pastor made his pastoral visitations at a Saturday auction on the main street. From the sideline, I engaged in small talk with townspeople. Again and again I heard their piety reflecting on their plight: "We didn't have it so bad. The family down the road had it worse." It was poignant that they seemed now to take for granted water in the church basement on Sunday morning. Such circumstance shapes ministry. It was important that their pastor was there, suffering with them.

I left North Dakota to visit Barb in Minnesota. She serves an open-country church. Canned goods were piled high around their Wednesday morning Bible study room, ready to be sent to flood victims miles away. "You've just come from North Dakota? How is it with the folks up there?" I felt like a living epistle: "I bring greetings from your sisters and brothers. . . . They thank God for your gifts and support. . . ."

I sat in on the Bible class, and choir practice, and on a pastor's text study. I went with Barb to visit an elderly gentleman. It was his birthday, and it would no doubt be his last. We shared home communion. Later I watched Barb sign confirmation certificates at the baptismal font. We visited a community family-living center where a parishioner works. "My pastor is here," she beamed, as she took us around to greet each staff member. It was clear that this was not the first time her pastor had visited her, or other members, in their places of ministry in daily life. Barb had been in this parish scarcely a year, but her ministry was far-reaching.

At the Thursday morning text study I had seen Kris, another of our seminary graduates. She invited me to stop by her place. So I did, visiting her large congregation in a nearby small city where she is in team ministry. That community is regaining its sense of identity after a devastating strike some years ago. Scars remain. As well as more questions. What is the role of a "pillar" congregation in ministering a word of Christ's healing hope?

Each place I went I was tempted to drive on down the road to make yet another visit. But not this time.

Jesus was always on the road. Christians, as the book of Acts says, are people on the way. The visitor has come and dwells among us. The Incarnate Christ liberates us to walk and to learn from the people we serve, and in so doing we participate in the living vocations of people we are privileged to encounter on the journey.

PART THREE
LIVING VOCATION

As members of the Body of Christ we are called to live out our vocations. What does vocation in Christ mean? Each of us, no matter what our gifts, our relationships, our occupations, is called to place all of our work—our successes as well as our failures—at the cross where we are made new in Christ's resurrection. We are forgiven, released, freed for new lives centered in Christ, ready to serve the neighbor. We are—all of us—called (*vocatio*) to ministry in daily life. Rooted in baptism, we are part of the *laos*, part of the priesthood of all believers. Because Jesus Christ is alive, we are called to life-giving ministry.

Vocation encompasses all that we do; yet not all that we do is automatically ministry. However, in each aspect of our ordinary lives there is potential for ministry. It is not the extraordinary events, sacrificial service, or miraculous works that are necessarily of the greatest significance. Christ can transform ordinary acts into life-changing events. Whether in steady long-term care or in a serendipitous encounter, we are empowered for faithful service. Whether in the church building, outside on the steps, on the city streets, or off in the hills, every place is holy ground when God's Word is spoken and Christ's care extended there.

All Christians are called to participate in Christ's mission every day of the week. Not just some are ministers; all Christian people (including priests, pastors, bishops, diaconal ministers) have daily lives. Within the call we all share, some are appointed (prepared, ordained, consecrated, commissioned) for particular leadership offices.[1] These particular ministries are part of the ministry of all the baptized, part of the all-encompassing ministry of the *laos*. The proper authority of office is not to dominate (lord it over), for only one is *"dominus,"* "Lord," and that is Jesus the Christ. Neither are members of a congregation to be primarily volunteers within the church, "helping out" the pastor. We are called outside the walls of the church into the mission of the church. Vocation, for all of us, includes not just paid occupations but also the volitional parts of our lives ("volunteer" in the true sense of the word). Our callings are based not on gender or class or race or status, but on gifts. We all have gifts and they differ from one person to another. Together we make up the Body of Christ.[2]

Just as gifts differ, so also do the specific needs of the worlds we enter, the individuals whose lives we touch. Letty Russell wrote, "The gospel is good news to people only when it speaks concretely to their particular needs of liberation. For instance, it is no help to tell the blind woman that she can walk. Good news for the blind must deal with changing the

101

oppressed situation of blindness."[3] The good news relates directly to the specific human predicament. Discerning that correlation is central to caring ministry. Where there is guilt, we are called to announce Christ's forgiveness. Where there are people in pain, we are called to ministries of care and health. Where people are torn apart by stress of daily existence, we are called to bring a wholeness centered and grounded in God. Where people are in chains—whether actual imprisonment or bondage to any power, obsession, or addiction that would enslave—we are called to vocations of liberation. Where people are lost, lonely, estranged, Christ gives shelter, inclusion, and community. We are called to minister in word and action the good news of life in forgiveness.

The whole people of God already are engaged in ministry. Marg Leegard, laywoman, farmer, writer, and lecturer from northwest Minnesota uses words as stark as prairie life itself to introduce us to that ministry. She receives a phone call that would call her away from her task. Ministry that day was not like she had thought it would be. It rarely is. The messiness of death and grief are beyond our expectations. Where do we expect to find the ministry of Word? From whom do we expect to receive ministry of care? Where does God expect to find us? Henri Nouwen said that cure without care is more harmful than helpful. Whose place is it anyway to care for the grieving? Word without deed, or deed without words won't do. We meet, and in the encounter, begin to entrust to each other the vocation to which we all are called.

We move from rural Minnesota to inner-city Detroit. Linda Ridgeway has lived with her family in the heart of Detroit for forty-two years. The story begins at Linda's retirement party; her daughter Angela now sees the scope of her mother's ministry in the people whose lives she has touched. Linda knows she is called to minister to her family and, with the same clear gospel witness, she extends her arms to young people in her church and her neighborhood. Linda's enduring faith in God is a beacon of hope in contexts of struggle. Such ministry is costly, but she continues to claim this as the place she needs to be, although she and her family could have fled the city years ago. Linda is convinced that Jesus can sustain us on our journey so that we can walk with young people each step of their journeys. What is central to ministry among children and youth and their families? How does the gospel empower youth faced with life-and-death decisions? How do we minister for a lifetime? This chapter is longer than most; it encompasses Linda's ministry over forty-six years, showing a commitment to youth from grade school into adulthood.

Rhonda Hanisch knows how to seize the moment. She viewed the lean times of rural economic problems as an opportunity to raise up the gifts of all the people. How does one lead a congregation in a healthy approach to stewardship? As part of her ongoing stewardship approach—not in opposition to or even detracting from it—she determined to help empower people to discover how they might grow. A seemingly simple plan called for trusting God, God's gifts, themselves, and one another. Deeper questions involve a congregation's view of ministry beyond their own needs. When a congregation has budget cuts to make, what is the first thing to go? How are congregations tempted to divorce budget decisions from gospel action? And how does one engage people in biblical study to empower their action? Leaders in mission are called to help a congregation live their vocation in the fullest sense of that word, for their own sakes and for the sake of those beyond the church walls.

Sandy Berg-Holte sees a mission field in her own backyard. Living vocation in the name of the Christ who had no place to lay his head leads Sandy to minister among forgotten rural homeless women and their children. Who will do this work? No one's work is everyone's vocation. Private lives become a public challenge. Thousands of people, not unlike ourselves, may at some time in their lives be within a paycheck of two of being homeless. When a woman who has never earned a paycheck needs to flee an abusive house, what will she do? Without shelter, where will she go? And do you then acquire the name, "problem"? Why do we keep hidden that which people consider shameful? Or is it the church that should be ashamed of choosing to ignore these societal wounds? Homelessness anywhere, whether in rural areas, urban centers, among war refugees, or after a natural disaster, requires a communal, holistic approach to ministry. Sandy is a leader who helps weave new lives of opportunity, responsibility, and community.

Pastors have come to use the term, "a ministry of presence," particularly in clinical pastoral education, as a healthy alternative to trying to "fix" people's lives, something human ministers cannot do. But a ministry of presence should not be equated with a passive, disinterested stance. A call to live our vocation of being present with Christ's love includes listening perceptively, waiting with and walking alongside people, and, at the right moment, speaking good news. Maryann Morgenstern's style of ministry embraces the interruptions. She has learned to understand the people of the high plains of eastern Montana. And they have learned to find her. The Spirit breathes new life into ordinary encounters. How do we learn to read the context, to hear the call to ministry in the interruptions? Through a child's persistence? In teenage tears? At the front door of the church?

Sister Mary Owen Haggerty delights in being a parish health minister literally to the entire parish. The experienced Roman Catholic nun serves a Lutheran and a Methodist congregation. How does living out our vocation call us across old boundaries? Sister Mary Owen believes health ministry is a good place to start. By giving attention to members of two congregations, their families, and sometimes their neighbors, she is helping to increase the health and well-being of the entire community. She listens to ordinary questions of people home from the hospital, of those entering the "assisted living" state of life, and of those who don't know how to cope. She listens, offers some specific medical information, and guides people to live more wisely. She brings a sense of well-being, even to confusing, conflicted lives. How do we bring good news from one to another? How do we minister to those who fall between the cracks? How might we lead in ways that increase the health of an entire community?

Our final chapter in Part Three is about the vocation of crossing congregational boundaries in another way. Is a congregation still a congregation when they don't have their "own" pastor? A church body has a vocation of helping all congregations not only survive but thrive. When Kathryn Bielfeldt's name was suggested to a congregation nine years ago, the bishop's office invited the people to venture into what was unknown to them. In receiving Kathy's leadership, the congregation took what could have been viewed as a handicapping condition and turned it into empowerment for sharing ministry. But where does sharing end? Next this congregation was asked to share their leader with other congregations who don't have a pastor. Across this land, congregations struggle with identity and call to mission. How can they live out their vocation as people of God in this place with what they see as limited gifts? How can their handicaps of smaller population and limited resources—"We're not the church we used to be"—become assets? That question will move us to the final part of this book: nurturing community.

Notes

1. Ephesians 4:11, "some would be apostles, some prophets, some evangelists, some pastors and teachers" is set within Ephesians 4:1-16. We have "one baptism." The appointment of specific positions is "to equip the saints for the work of ministry" (v. 12). The whole body together, when it is working properly, promotes the body's growth in building itself up in love.

2. See also Romans 12 and 1 Corinthians 12.

3. Letty M. Russell, *Human Liberation in a Feminist Perspective: A Theology* (Philadelphia: Westminster, 1974), p. 53.

CHAPTER THIRTEEN

Ordinary Roles: The Ministry of Word and Care

Marj Leegard

Called to places where rifts have isolated but a community cares, we learn new roles of ministry. Marj takes us right to the middle of things: the granary, grief, and groups of neighbors. That's where she found herself. Or is it that Jesus finds us there?

It was late on a hot summer afternoon in harvest time. The phone was ringing and phones were not portable to the flower patch. I ran into the house and grabbed the receiver. It was our next-door neighbor to the south, Hilda. She said, "Come right away! Herb is in the grain bin. I think he is dead." She hung up. I ran out to the car. My husband was coming into the yard. He jumped off the combine and asked where I was going. I said, "Oh, come. I'll tell you on the way."

There are neighbors and there are neighbors. We weren't very friendly with this couple. They were older. They hadn't lived here very long. There were good reasons and a piece of land and a line fence and a wrong. But they were in trouble.

We parked and went into the granary. She was right. Her husband was dead. She had called the ambulance. My husband, Jerome, went out to the field to tell the harvest crew to quit. The ambulance came howling into the yard. While the sheriff and the coroner were talking to Hilda, I went to the house to call our pastor. He was new, not only to our parish but new to ordained ministry. I told him there had been an accident and asked if he remembered how he had driven to our farm last Sunday. "Just turn south instead of north at that last corner," I said.

I went out to the group standing by the ambulance. The sheriff was asking questions. Hilda did not give him time to write the answers. She wanted them to hurry, but there was no reason to hurry. I helped Hilda across the yard and into the house. We went through the living room and up the stairs to the bathroom. I had thought sometimes of what I would do in a situation like this. Always I imagined myself beautifully dressed. Not in old jeans with dirt on the knees from the petunia bed. The one I would comfort was never violently ill. This was no dream. My stomach wrenched and knotted and I willed it to be still so that I could hold her as she got rid of sobs and moans and stomach contents. Just as things would calm down and we began to wash ourselves, the whole process began again.

"The Ordinary Things Were Being Done"

We finally came down the steps and there were some of the neighbors in the living room. I thought it would be a good time for me to leave, but she clung to me as she was being embraced and comforted by each new arrival. When one friend stood and began to say good-bye, Hilda, in all her distress, could not forget her duty as hostess. "You must stay. We will make some coffee." Each friend in turn had the same answer, "Oh, we had coffee." They pointed past the dining room, in the general direction of the kitchen.

One group came in carrying a plate of supper for Hilda and one for me. We were not hungry but it was a good feeling to know that someplace the ordinary things were being done. I asked Hilda if she had called her children. "Yes, I did," she said. "I called our son after I called the ambulance. Just before I called you. He is going to let the others know." He lived four hours away. It looked as if I would be here for a while.

I wondered where our pastor was. People kept coming. The embraces and shared tears mingled with the short phrases of comfort. "God will take care of you." "We will pray for you." "Herb was a good man." "My husband is milking your cows so don't worry about that." "I know but I really don't know. My husband was sick for so long. This is different." "In just a little while your son will be here. That will help." And all the time I am trying to find words that will dry the tears, but there are no words. So I just sat beside her and let her hold my hand and lean on me.

People came and went and the daylight turned to dusk. The last group of neighbors gathered children and purses and were gone. A car drove in. "Oh. That's Bud." She began to sob with her new realization of the pain. I held her as we stood together in the middle of the room. Her son walked in and our pastor was behind him.

"It's about time," I muttered to myself. The four of us clung together and tried to wipe our noses and our tears. Pastor asked if we would like to pray and on hearing an affirmative answer, he lead us, while we were still standing in a tight little group, by praying that God would be particularly close in these next days. He thanked God for friends and family who had already gathered and for the safety of those still on the way. He asked God to quiet the questions in our hearts until we were strong enough to understand. And then the "amen" with the question, "Will you be all right alone now? I will come back in the morning." Hilda thanked him for coming and assured him that they would get along until tomorrow.

We walked outside together, Pastor and I. Jerome had left our car when he went home to milk our cows. The yellow glow from the yard light shone on the damp car top. The air was now cool. Pastor put his hands on my car top and put his head down on his hands. "I blew it," he said.

"Blew it? What did you do?" I asked with a good bit of impatience included. I wanted to ask, "How am I supposed to do what I don't know *how* to do while you are off doing something else when I asked you to come here?" But I did not ask. Maybe the church council could point out to him that he should come when he is called. He stayed beside the car, his head down. Finally I asked, not for my information but to comfort him, "What happened?"

His voice was muffled. "I've never been called like this before. We had only one accident in the congregation while I was interning. People called the pastor when they were ready to make funeral arrangements. I didn't know what to do. When I came I helped the ambulance people and the sheriff get Mr. Norby out of the grain bin. Then I talked with the sheriff about what had happened. You and Mrs. Norby were just going into the house when I came."

"That was hours ago," I said.

"Yes, I know. The time went by so fast. The afternoon coffee dishes were still on the kitchen table so I washed them up. I was a cook in the army so I know my way around kitchens. I made a pot of coffee and people started coming. They all stopped in the kitchen. They had brought plates of cookies and cake. I gave them coffee and they sat around the kitchen table and asked me what had happened. I thought it would be better if I explained it out there. I took the cookies and squares of cake and added them to the serving platters. While we talked I washed their plates so that I could return them. Then the next groups began bringing sandwiches and salads and I made supper for the men who were doing the chores. I made supper for you." He looked at me. I nodded. So that's where supper came from.

"People brought so much food that I labeled all the containers with names and filled the fridge and then wrapped what could be frozen and found the freezer for that. I made a list of all the people who came and what they brought because I thought she would want to know."

"I Had Just Assumed . . ."

The things Pastor was busy with in the kitchen were the things we women always had to do in places where people gathered. I had just assumed that there were women in the kitchen. It was the natural, ordinary way to do things. When there is a great upheaval, nothing is ordinary. I could imagine the people in the community checking with one another. "Who was that man in the kitchen?" "I think that is the new pastor over at Richwood." "No! Can't be. I mean the one with the khaki pants and the old white shirt with the sleeves rolled up." "Well, maybe I'm wrong. Clerical collars make a difference." It takes them time to figure it all out.

> *"What makes you think the gospel was not in the living room?"*

I said, "Thank you for all you did." He looked at me and put his head down again. "I should have been in the living room with the gospel," he said.

At that time I had never heard of the ministry of the laity. I never thought of ministry as part of my calling as a Christian woman, but I knew in the depths of my being that something was wrong here.

"What makes you think that the gospel was not in the living room?" I asked.

No answer. His head remained down.

"Well, the gospel was there. Maybe it is hard to recognize. No person in her right mind would do the things I did today just because I live down the road. I cleaned her up and I mopped the bathroom because I was called to do that. People came when they would much rather stay away. Who needs to see tears and fear and worry? We could send a card, you know. Maybe we couldn't explain *why* it happened. I don't know where to look for that in the Bible. She didn't ask me *why*. She only asked me to stay with her. I think that is gospel, too." By this time I was so upset I was crying.

Now he had to lift his head and comfort me.

"I'm sorry," he said. "I never thought of that. The gospel was in the living room. I wish I had gone in there, too."

Now I was really upset. "This is possibly the only time people ever will see you doing those kitchen things. We women do that all the time. Look wherever you go. Someone is washing up and setting out and inviting to the table. When we do that the gospel is in the kitchen, too." There was nothing more to say.

He walked to his car and I got in mine and we left.

I came to my neighbor's home not knowing what to do and resenting the call. Pastor came not knowing anything about mutual ministry: clergy and laity together. Neither of us made any connection between the kitchen and the living room. I did not know what I knew until I reacted to his genuine sorrow for his perceived failure. We learned together.

CHAPTER FOURTEEN

Ordinary Neighbors:
Youth Ministry

Linda L. Ridgeway

No one is too old or too young to minister among youth. In your neighborhood, where are the young people? Linda believes we need to go with them every step of the journey; no place is too dangerous. This chapter is a collage of first-person stories and letters, a panoramic view of the three generations Linda has touched with the gospel. All these years she has lived in the same, ordinary house on 30th Street in Detroit. Here is an extraordinary challenge for us all.

This story begins at the retirement party for Linda Ridgeway who worked for an automotive firm for twenty-two years. Angela Ridgeway Patterson, an accountant in the field of health services, writes about her mother:

Angela Speaks:

I'm the second child of seven children and from my first knowledge of her, my mom has been a youth director in our local church. She enjoys bike riding, hiking, picnics, competitive outdoor games, swimming, summer camp, and winter camp. You name it and Mom is there organizing and participating.

Many times, as a child, I selfishly wondered why we always "took along" other kids on our family trips. Couldn't I have her all to myself? She gave me her attention, but she also took time to be attentive to other children.

This year, at her retirement party, I realized what a tremendous impact her life has had on those she "took along." Two-thirds of those in attendance were young adults who remarked that she not only took them along to organized activities, but also took them along in her heart. Much of what they learned from the Bible was by reading her life. Some, like the prodigal son (Luke 15:11-32), had taken a journey into the far country, and returned to say, "When I came to myself, I knew the way back to God." Youth ministries had planted the seed of a repentant heart.

At age sixty-two Mom is still the youth director and children's choir director at her church. I asked her what has kept her going for the past forty years of ministry. In response she pulled a tattered piece of paper from her purse, a note written to her by seven-year-old Mary, "I love you forever in my heart. She will love me like I love her." Mary's mother is a single parent, currently enrolled in college. Mom had been mentor for Mary's mother when she was a child and Mary's mother now participates in youth ministry, too, so the righteous seed will continue.

Two years ago, when the sale of illegal drugs at the community playground was increasing and it was obvious the drug dealers were recruiting younger and younger children to sell the drugs, youth ministries expanded to include a program called, "Miracles on 30th Street." In the spring, Mom and her kids plant flowers, and carry

> *Youth Ministry is a labor of love and service sustained by the Spirit of God.*

water from a neighbor's home to nurture the plants all spring and summer. As the flowers grow, community interest grows into efforts to keep the grounds clean and drug free. While Mom and her "kids" are working there, the older youth, themselves now drug dealers, apologize for their foul language and set down their bottles to open their arms for a hug from "Mom."

Not all of Mom's stories are successes. Some seeds of love fall on thorny hearts and no positive results can be seen immediately; but someone will water the seed, and God will give the increase. That promise keeps us all going! Immediate results and fast solutions cannot be the yardstick for measuring success in ministry. Youth ministry is a labor of love and service sustained by the Spirit of God.

About eight months ago, I rededicated my life of service to Jesus Christ. Guess what my assignment is. Youth director! I've been married fourteen years and my husband has often said, "I'm trying to give you time to grow up and act your age." My response to him is, "Look at my mother!" So I'm the next "big kid" to have the privilege of "taking others along" with my own twelve-year-old son, Jaret, in activities and in my heart. And we will be the Bible others read.

> May those who sow in tears
> reap with shouts of joy.
> Those who go out weeping,
> bearing the seed for sowing,
> shall come home with shouts of joy,
> carrying their sheaves. (Psalm 126:5-6)

Linda Speaks:

My family and I have lived on 30th Street in Detroit for forty-two years. When I'm asked why our family stays in the inner city, I say it's because we have a mission here. We have suffered some adverse situations, but I think this is where I belong.

Youth ministry is a mixture of formal and informal work. When I was sixteen, I started a youth choir and youth ministry grew out of that. I would take the youth to rallies and expose them to other Christian leaders and messages. As a result of that beginning, I'm working on my third generation of children. Many of the youth I worked with have gone on to become pastors and deacons and lay leaders in their congregations. Most still live in the Detroit area, and we keep in touch.

There are some things you don't know about when you are sixteen. I'm now sixty-two; that's forty-six years of doing youth ministry in the same congregation and neighborhood. The area where we concentrate is actually just in a six-block radius. Many people have come and gone in all those years, especially renters. But many of the senior citizens, the retirees, continue to live here.

Years ago Greg was a young boy in our neighborhood. He's now married and has children. His wife, Tina, has training in youth evangelism, and she came over recently to help us hold a five-day club on the playground on 30th Street. Across the street, some of the young men were selling drugs. I said, "We're going to have a five-day club here and we need some help." So they helped clean up the playground.

My heart aches for the youth because the demon of drugs is powerful today. Too many people messing up; not enough cleaning up. Youth need Jesus Christ in their lives so they can resist. Some come from solid homes, and from churchgoing families, but the drug culture is very strong. However, remember the darker it is, the brighter the light of Christ is.

Greg is one of four elders at the church where Sims is leading a ministry. I've known Sims for over thirty years. During the 1960s he was listening to groups that called for hatred of Whites and he was trying to reconcile his anger with his Christian faith. It was hard for him to hear, "Be kind and love those that despitefully use you" when as an African American he had to go to those White people and ask for a job and be rejected. One day he came over and I shared with him that if anyone is in Christ, that one is a new creature and all old things have passed away. He said, "I knew it had to be this way." The work of Christ in you produces a new behavior.

Sims has been a fireman now for almost thirty years. He was hired just when Blacks were first able to be hired by the fire department. He's also been a pastor leading a church for twelve years and works a lot with youth. He knows that reaching young African American men from the ages of twenty-five to thirty-two is a particular challenge, because of the racism and economic injustice in our society.

You Need to Love One Youth at a Time

I really appreciate the partnership of Tina, and I especially value her expertise. I feel a burden for the community, but the responsibility is more than one person can carry. Together we distribute fliers (with tape on them so they can be put on refrigerators) from my house up and down 30th Street to the expressway. That's only about a four-block area. We talked with the parents. The first day thirty children came and by the end of the week we had sixty children at the five-day club.

In youth ministry you have to walk the streets; you have to get out and get involved. There can be no impact without contact. You have to talk to people and touch them, hug them both emotionally and physically. You have to walk up on porches and knock on doors. You can start a Bible class in your backyard and simply invite young people to come and then have each one invite one more. The key is reaching out and helping youth reach out to one another. I challenge them. One year a child brought twenty-four other children. You need to love one youth at a time but I also go for the numbers. Why do all that preparation and have only twelve people when you could reach 120? My goal is to help youth become involved with the Word so they have something to give back to other youth. Some come and stay on the sidelines, but those who come to church, come looking. When they begin to see the Lord working through them with younger children, it encourages them to study the Word even more. They are growing as they are going; growing as they give.

Neighborhood outreach is the mission of the church. Make sure no young person goes through your church without knowing they're loved, that they're special. Christians come to the church and refuel, but ministry is outside the walls. From the very beginning and to this day, the children's choir essentially is evangelistic outreach. Children come because their friends invite them. And even if the parents at first come only when their children sing, many eventually come into the church to stay. You have to begin youth ministry early. Bible study, prayer, praise, and service are essential. We begin early learning how to pray at choir rehearsal by going around the circle and becoming acquainted with talking to God. "God's listening to our voice," I say, and the children begin to break in with things for which they want to thank God. Once involved in choir, many of them sing throughout their teenage years.

On the second Sunday of each month we involve the teenagers in drama and puppeteer work. They take on a whole range of leadership roles: greeting visitors, reading lessons, leading prayers. Adolescents don't want exposure; but on the other hand, they do. "Look at me, but don't look." They need very much for us to look at them. That Sunday they stay after church for a youth rally. We prepare Black history materials for them to read, play upbeat music, and involve them in service projects. When I graduated from high school years ago, we hadn't yet heard of African American history. Now we know truth is in the truth-telling. We can't wait for others to tell it; we cannot let it not be told. It must be repeated for those who will come after us who will not have lived through the experience. So it is with the stories of any oppressed people, the marginalized—those invisible by class, race, or gender.

Most of our youth stay in church activities until they are seventeen or eighteen. Sometimes the older youth step outside the church for awhile. And some of the older people don't have patience for this sustaining ministry. They may say, "I'm not cut out for that." But they will support the youth ministry with food. I could probably get more help from the other adults if I asked. I'm not totally alone, but sometimes I feel alone. There are so many demands and so many needs: planning, designating, and follow-through.

We have to invite people to Christ in spite of the inadequacies of the church. The slaves looked past the Christian church to accept Jesus. How do we invite people to faith? We must listen very closely to hear their pain in order to speak about Christ to that deepest need.

Words for Rebecca:

While Linda was telling her story, the doorbell rang. It was a young woman coming to pick up a letter of reference Linda had written. Linda said:

I've known Rebecca since she was a child. She didn't have much affection shown to her as a teenager. She married and got involved with her husband in alcohol. He then left her with four children. She was later arrested for carrying a concealed weapon. That was cleared up, but it will take $500 to expunge the arrest from her record. Life has kicked her around, but she's strong in the Word and has her life together now. She raised her children and they have gone on to college and are doing well. She wants to start a day care center, and needs a letter of reference.

The Letter of Reference

This is to advise that I have been personally acquainted with Rebecca Jones from adolescence through adulthood. As a youth she was energetic and showed enthusiasm for and was punctual in attending scheduled activities. She was very much a team player.

Progressing through adulthood, in her marriage and parenting Rebecca exhibited perseverance, dedication, and resilience. When the "going gets tough" she maintains faith in the promises of God and seeks God's strength and guidance. She has given love and nurture to her family. She and her children make positive contributions in the community as role models who seek education, employment, and service to others."

Linda Ridgeway, Director of Youth Ministry

Churches Need to Open Their Doors

The goal is to help youth stay connected with God. Many, when they can, move out of the neighborhood, out to the Seven Mile Road area. They see folks able to have money and cars and that seems like the goal worth striving for. Those who stay in the neighborhood are tempted to seek the money the drug dealers promise, and some adopt them as their role models. But if some of us stay here in the neighborhood, we can serve as alternative role models. I want to strengthen the youth so they can survive in this culture without being drawn in—so they can stay and give something back. The goal is not just to prepare the youth to tunnel out of the inner city, but to work together to take down the walls that divide us. We have to prepare youth to live in their neighborhood or to go beyond into the broader world. Many have gone on to college and now live and serve across the country. Those who stay here need something about which they can be proud. They need respect. The gospel gives them a sense of worth. The God of the universe places worth on them, loves them so much God would send God's only Son. When your back is against the wall, there is God. Sometimes you wonder how God can help them even while you believe God will never leave them or forsake them. You see them struggle and know they are making harmful choices and facing a brick wall. Sometimes someone comes along to give them a boost to get over the wall. And then they stumble and fall again. Sometimes you become very discouraged.

When we work on the playground and I wave to the young men selling drugs, they wave back. But I need to talk to them one-on-one. And we need more adults involved in order to do that effectively. We ask other churches in the area to come, but many don't want to extend themselves into the neighborhood. They try to protect their own turf. I know most youth leaders are wearing ten hats already, but if we just all came outdoors together, the results would be amazing.

There is a youth network in Detroit, and we work together ecumenically. Youth for Christ moved out and took their program to the suburbs. But the group we have now helps us do some things together that our church alone couldn't afford, like sponsoring an all-nighter of intramural sports at Eastern Michigan University. The White churches that have kept their doors open have shared resources and we're doing youth ministry together. The church that doesn't open its doors to others will have to close its own.

Of course I don't stay connected with all the youth as they grow up. Some I may not see for ten years. Many are still living their faith and we are connected in Christ. I may or may not be able to follow them, but our family has stayed here, so they can find us. When God connects us again we will have some really good times.

The youth and I have an especially good time around August 16th each year. That's my husband Booker's birthday. On the weekend closest to that day, "Big T" holds a cookout. We have two vacant lots next to our house that he manicures so he can set up a big tent. Sometimes two hundred people show up. And they keep coming. They hear about the party—all the way to the expressway—and stop by. He cooks plenty of food and doesn't turn anyone away—even if he has to cut some chicken pieces in two. The food always stretches as far as it should. It creates community.

Our family also has faced the struggles of the neighborhood. We are not immune. With family members in the prison system, I've felt the pain of not being able to take them home with me when I was used to them sleeping in their own beds upstairs. I would go to bed and wait to hear their footsteps. You know what can happen in prison, but you come to a point when you say to the Lord, "I can't fall apart every time the circumstances change." And when the fear comes back again, hope endures with a confidence that God, who gives peace, is still on the throne. God's love cares too much to give up. God is with our youth wherever they are, even in prison. I had to believe that God is God and takes care of our sons, even when they are in prison.

We have been tempted to move to some place where it would be safer, but where can you go? God has proven God's faithfulness. Sometimes I've questioned, but instead of taking a victim's attitude, I have to continue to trust in God's love.

Some of the neighborhood youth grow up and become part of the prison system. Prisons are being filled with Black men, so they will be full when private enterprise ownership takes over. It's a lucrative business. Our children are not safe on the streets; I fear even more for their safety in prison. Still I hold the overriding conviction that they are covered by the blood of Jesus.

Excerpts from Malcolm's Letters from Prison:

I have been crucified with Christ; and it is no longer I who live, but it is Christ who lives in me. And the life I now live in the flesh I live by faith in the Son of God, who loved me and gave himself for me. (Galatians 2:19-20)

As always, it was a blessing to receive your letter. I am thanking and praising God that you all are well. . . . You don't know how much a letter or a simple phone call means here in an atmosphere of much negativity and despair. . . . All in all, I thank God for God's grace and mercy. I know some would think that I am in a situation where I am fighting for my life (with the judicial system that seems to have a lock-them-up-and-throw-away-the-key mentality), but I look at it as my being the product of grace. So I don't worry about the outcome, because I know that God will use this situation, too. Our Bible Study group here is flourishing and men's lives are being changed. I welcome this calling wholeheartedly, regardless of the outcome of my case. I thank God for the privilege of being considered faithful to bring God's Word to men who are developing a thirst for the Word. . . . Continue to hold me up to God in your prayers as I will you." Malcolm.

Linda Speaks:

When young men are in prison we need to visit them. It's so important for families to keep in touch while they are away. Family members are not going to put their lives on hold, so there are some decisions to make. Prison pushes people apart just when they need each other. Family cohesiveness is severed. A society riddled with racism places additional burdens on families. It's hard when family members take different paths. They no longer understand one another. When a family member is released from prison, others no longer know the person who came home.

Part of our young adult ministry is simply keeping in touch. When young people come out of prison, it's hard to secure a job. They are in double jeopardy. If they have been convicted of a felony, they won't be hired; but if they don't mention their record, and the employer finds out about their conviction, they won't be able to stay. So we advise them to be honest and take their chances. You have to be with them through all stages of the journey.

While one young man was away, he completed two courses in addiction counseling. His letter to employers reads in part: "I wish to work in the field of substance abuse prevention, and am currently pursuing a bachelor's degree in addiction studies from the University of Detroit Mercy College. My long-range goal is to acquire a master's degree in psychology. In addition, I am pursuing certification as an addiction counselor." This young man presently is working with his father in his home improvement business. That's going well.

Believing the Word Will Bear Fruit

After all these years we have some current congregational struggles. Even though I and other women had been serving for many years, the pastor recently said, "Women keep silent; go home and ask your husband." Of course I don't need to say anything; my presence speaks. Anybody with influence has to put a lid on it. The pastor has taken the choir away from me. I felt that whatever contribution I made would go to his credit, but he doesn't see it that way. He doesn't want women having too much influence. I don't think he knows how to fix the situation he had caused. Many people are leaving the church. To me, the children are the issue, not him or his leadership. I will respond to the needs of the youth.

How is youth ministry in the inner city today different than it was thirty or forty years ago? It may have seemed like the good old days of baseball and apple pie. But, of course, that wasn't true. Many youth had problems then, and didn't get help; they acted out their struggles. Families today are more scattered. Youth are more susceptible, and there is a much greater proliferation of guns and drugs and anger.

In youth ministry you invest a lot of yourself in young people. Sometimes they go into the far country and don't come back. They stay there for awhile. You don't have them to help and come alongside; they remain in their struggle. But some do come back and together we reach out to the next generation.

One can feel heavy with bearing a lot of the burden, feeling the need to carry them. But I learned from a psychologist how not to let it drag me down, how to have some boundaries even while I still carry them on my heart. I had to learn to give it to the Lord, believing God is working in their lives even when I can't see it. God will send another traveler across their path. I have to believe the Word will bear fruit in their lives.

CHAPTER FIFTEEN

Ordinary Gifts:
The Ministry of Stewardship

Rhonda R. Hanisch

Wise congregations lead people to consider stewardship questions all year long. Rhonda tells of a particular approach when her congregation, though unable to continue its financial support, was unwilling to cut back on its commitment to mission. She drew on a parable, dared to risk, and confidently believed the community could meet the challenge.

My first call was to a congregation in a rural setting that had a worshiping attendance of seventy-five. This congregation enjoyed a mission partnership with three other ministry settings: a mission congregation, a prison congregation, and a university worshiping community. Financial support for these three mission partners had been a line item in the congregation's budget for years. However, due to ongoing rural economic problems, each year the budget became leaner and leaner until it appeared that cutting off the mission partnerships was imminent. No one wanted to make the cut. Nevertheless, tough budget decisions demand sacrifices.

At the November council meeting where the decision was to be made, we searched and discussed various ways to remain supportive of our mission partners. Sacrificing mission went against the grain of these courageous prairie people. I suggested we support our mission partners by being in mission ourselves, using a concept that had its origin in Matthew

25:14-30. The parable reveals God's trust in us, so, I said, let's trust God and participate in the work God has given us to do, which in this instance was to support our mission partners. We would take the parable of the talents and put it into the hands of the people of the congregation.

> "Stewardship is about living the good news."

In the parable of the talents the master gives a fortune over into the hands of three slaves and leaves them to do with it as they will. These are slaves, not investment brokers; they are not savvy in the intricacies of financial management. Yet they are the ones the master trusts with ridiculously huge amounts of money; one talent is the equivalent of fifteen years' wages. The master seems unconcerned about making a profit. Instead, he is concerned about whether or not these slaves will return his trust, and the master is willing to go to tremendous lengths to find out.

Sharing the Project

God has turned over to us the greatest treasure in all of heaven and earth: the good news of Jesus Christ. God is concerned with our returning God's trust and bringing Christ to people. If this sounds a lot like evangelism, well and good, because evangelism and stewardship are two fingers of the same hand, the hand of mission. Stewardship is not merely about money. Stewardship is about living the good news. We share Christ with people in the way we live our lives, including the way we manage our money.

In the council meeting we read the parable and discussed it at length. We examined the risk God takes in entrusting the good news to us. We talked about stewardship and how we as church leaders can best teach stewardship in daily life. We withheld making a decision until our next meeting. This gave each of us time to pray about the proposal, to pray for our mission partners and for God's wisdom.

The time between the November and the December council meetings was electric. Lots of conversations occurred at the coffee shop, the post office, and the gas station, not to mention in the church itself. We were considering a risky adventure. It's not every congregation that gives money away with no strings attached. The church had not done it that way before. The concerns were legitimate. "What if the venture fails?" "What if no one does anything with the money?" "What if we make more money than we used to give our mission partners? Do we keep the difference?"

When the council met in December, the members geared up to go forward with the proposal. The concerns were heard and addressed. We prayed and then cut the line item from the budget that represented our financial support for our mission partners. At the annual congregational meeting we proposed that we join our partners in mission through the "5, 2, 1 Talent Project."

We filled the envelopes with "seed" money, either $5, $2, or $1. Obviously, this amount of money does not come close to the value of a talent; however, the purpose of the project was neither to replicate the parable, nor merely to make money. The purpose was to bring steward-ship and mission into daily thought, word, and deed. Enough envelopes were filled to allow for all those in worship on a given Sunday to receive one, with a few extras for those who may have missed that Sunday. Just as each slave in the parable was included and received the talents from the master, so too, everyone in worship was encouraged to take an envelope: older folks, younger folks, visitors, and members alike. Participation in God's kingdom is not limited; therefore, no one was to be excluded from this project.

We took the "seed" money from our memorial savings account with the understanding that the "seed" would be returned before any monies gar-nered were dispersed. We continually emphasized that this was not a fund-raiser. It was not a competition. The goal was to express one's faith, one's trust in God, through the exercise of one's particular gifts and talents.

We gave suggestions for what to do with the money. We also encour-aged people to use their imaginations. People could pool their resources to facilitate partnerships in mission. The "ingathering of the talents" would include not only the increase of the seed money, if any, but also a recount-ing of what was done with it. The recounting would remain anonymous.

The project ran from May through October. On the spring day that the "seed" money was "planted," the Sunday school students held their final program, and so the church was full of worshipers. The last Sunday in October seemed appropriate for an ingathering of talents; a harvest cele-bration of sorts. Following the initial sermon on the parable of time and talents, a reverse offering took place. The ushers carried the offering plates full of money envelopes and passed them among the people. Included in the envelopes was a note, briefly describing the project, the task of a stew-ard, the scripture referent, and the date of the ingathering.

On the Sunday in May, $336 in talent money was dispersed. The tearing open of envelopes could be heard throughout the congregation, a sure sign of excitement. Throughout the summer, talent fairs cropped up from time to time, allowing participants to "increase" their talent. Most folks par-ticipated in the talent fairs, bringing their baked and canned goods, craft items, and fresh produce. A few others kept their projects a secret. It was a summer of intrigue and delight as the project perked along.

On the last Sunday in October, the church was full once more with excited worshipers. Following another sermon on the parable, and after singing the hymn "We Give Thee But Thine Own," everyone walked to the chancel. Tears of joy glistened on many cheeks as the ingathering of the talents was placed upon the altar. After the service, congregation members and visitors alike spoke of their appreciation for the opportunity to bear witness to their faith in this manner. Many told of feeling the presence and power of the Holy Spirit. They said they felt the Master say, "Well done, good and trustworty slave . . . enter into the joy of your master."

With the seed money returned to the memorial fund, the net increase from the project was $2,283.27. What a privilege to write the letters to our mission partners informing them of the reason we were sending them so much more money than we had in the past! The project changed the congregation's mission vision. All agreed to continue the mission partnerships using this project.

Extending the Project

I have since moved from that congregation to a congregation with an average worshiping attendance of about four hundred. The "5, 2, 1 Talent Project" has worked just as well in this larger congregation. A key blessing of the project is the joy people experience in putting their imaginations and talents to work for the mission of the church. The project provides on-the-job training in stewardship for people of all ages. People shared stories of how the project became a part of daily discussion at the dinner table.

Even children got involved. Two boys bought seeds for mini-maize, raised and harvested the crop, and sold the ears for autumnal table decorations. Another bought construction paper and made and sold airplanes of differing designs. One little girl bought a coloring book, colored the pages and then sold them as refrigerator art.

One family pooled its resources, went to antique stores and bought jewelry, cleaned it, and sold it to collectors in other parts of the country. What to do with only $1? One person bought gasoline and hired himself out to mow lawns on Saturday afternoons. Another enterprising person bought nightcrawlers, went fishing, and sold the catch. People invested their talents in things they enjoyed doing, learning in the process that being a steward in God's kingdom is not drudgery, but is, in fact, delightful.

People not privy to the project often would ask congregational members what they were doing and why. This provided members with an opportunity to talk about the parable, the project, and their faith. They enjoyed telling others about what they were learning in the process. Word of the project has spread to other congregations; requests for information about it continue to come in.

People in places that used the project primarily to raise money discovered the project did not work very well. The "5, 2, 1 Talent Project" is not a quick fix for budget woes. It's a mission project. The parable clearly shows that making money is not the point. The point is doing mission.

Exploring the Potential

The focus of stewardship is often money, giving, pledging, and tithing. Stewardship does encompass more than our money and what we do with it; however, I believe we also can use the narrow focus to proclaim the gospel.

Jesus talks a lot about money, using it in his parables about the kingdom. Stewardship needs to proclaim the gospel, that in Christ we die to self and are raised to newness of life. Nothing has a stronger hold on our old self than does money. The old self is addicted to money, and so clings to it for life, or "until death do us part." Obviously we can't cure ourselves, but, because of Jesus Christ, we can be in recovery! One step in that recovery is to put Scripture to work in the hands of the people.

The project has tremendous potential for mission both locally and globally. One needs only to dare. At a conference pastors' meeting not long ago, an assistant to the bishop explained that the synod was going to spend some of its budget to bring in stewardship experts. These experts would teach congregations how to do stewardship. I suggested that the synod give the money to congregations along with the challenge of the parable of the talents. I argued that the baptized already know how to do stewardship; they simply need to be trusted as the master trusted his slaves by investing enormous amounts in them. Sure, there are slothful slaves, people who willfully neglect the responsibility God has invested in them. Yet if God can risk the gospel by giving it to the likes of all the baptized, why can't churches risk a few dollars to be invested in all the believers, rather than in only the experts? Depending upon "experts" squashes the zeal and zest for mission in the rest of us and transforms us into apathetic pew potatoes. The bishop's assistant looked at me as though I were a bit crazy.

God's vision is all encompassing. God pours out the Holy Spirit upon all the baptized. Each is given the gift of the Spirit for mission, for building up the Body of Christ. God's grace is indeed extraordinary, and can be experienced in the ordinary ministry of the baptized. Scripture evinces the power of the ordinary ministry of all believers. The disciples were by no means experts, and yet the Acts of the Apostles reveals the extraordinary mission in which they boldly engaged.

I cannot help wondering what difference there might be in mission support and stewardship development if we took Scripture seriously and trusted the people of God to do what God requires of them. These days, we all need to be sent out boldly to do the work of the Master for the Master.

CHAPTER SIXTEEN

Ordinary Families: The Ministry of Transition

Sandy Berg-Holte

Sandy describes a ministry to families whose needs may go unrecognized. Who are the invisible people in your backyard? Sandy shows us real people with names and stories. This transitional housing ministry plants seeds of hope through listening, supporting, and empowering people with respect and self-worth.

It's something that is not talked about.

It's something that remains invisible to most.

It's rural homelessness. Most think homelessness is only an urban issue. People hold images of people sleeping on sidewalks, under bridges, in warehouses, or in condemned buildings in cities. We have no visual images of rural homelessness. It remains hidden.

Rural Homelessness

CornerStone Ministries serves homeless women and their children in rural Minnesota. In some ways the work, the ministry, is simple and self-explanatory. CornerStone is a supportive transitional housing program, the only transitional housing program within Volunteers of America, a Christian nonprofit social service agency. We offer affordable and decent housing to those in need.

This is a ministry, but a ministry without walls. We have no church building. We worship monthly at CornerStone, but worship is just one part of a much bigger picture of what goes on here in Christ's name. Supportive services include child care in our licensed child care center, transportation from volunteer or county drivers, information and resources for counseling, education, and local employment or job readiness experiences.

Each family comes with its own story. Since Brenda's significant other had been in jail, she and their four children had been living with friends and family, moving from house to house for the past three weeks. Daily life was becoming more stressful and less manageable. Because of this family crisis, Brenda lost her job and the family's income. The past year had been chaotic; the family had moved four times. Brenda came to CornerStone with clothes for her and the children, a few toys, and a car with over two hundred thousand miles on it that broke down within a week of her arrival.

We welcome each homeless family and assist each member in meeting immediate needs. We offer a time and a place to stabilize one's family, to get one's bearings, and to decide on some attainable goals. Our mission is to support families on the path to self-sufficiency.

As the residents come to know that they will be

Carol was here for six months before she felt safe enough to share the truth of her life.

treated with care and respect, they share more of their story and their struggles. Trust and respect are essential to personal growth. As the resident's sense of safety grows, she becomes willing to risk new choices and new behaviors. She becomes willing to look at her past and its patterns, and then, to begin letting go of obstacles and attitudes that she has outgrown.

Carol was here for six months before she felt safe enough to share the truth of her life experience as a person with learning disabilities. She had always known she was different. It was a huge step for her to name and claim that part of her life. Now she didn't have to hide the challenges she faces. Now she could ask for help and resources, and she is discovering that they are available. In the midst of her growth I am learning, through her, what it means to live with ordinary daily challenges. She is my teacher.

CornerStone also hosts a food shelf that serves the wider community, a clothing closet, and a domestic shelf with household items and supplies. Our nine apartments in three large triplex houses, each in a rural wooded setting, are furnished, including appliances. Families can stay for up to two years. Some choose to stay just a few months to get their bearings and get their feet on the ground; others choose to stay longer.

Betty and her three preschool children were residents at CornerStone for about four months because her previous housing had been condemned. After looking at her options, Betty chose to enroll in business school, started computer programming classes, and then decided to relocate closer to her schooling.

Val and her two children, however, stayed the entire twenty-four months. She liked CornerStone, the local community, her children's school, and her congregation. Val then chose to find subsidized housing in the local community to provide continuity for her and her children.

Homelessness is not simple and there are no simple answers. In the 1980s it was thought that affordable housing would solve the problem. Providing housing without case management did not lead to the desired self-sufficiency. Case management, support, and follow-through are necessary. Child care and transportation are crucial. Education and training beyond a high school diploma or GED is needed to find employment that will support a family in our state. Women come with different amounts of education—from having completed only eighth grade to having obtained a few college credits.

These women don't look any different from women in one's congregation, but they have multiple and complex issues—including solo parenting and being the sole economic support of the family—without much social support from relatives and friends. One common thread in the lives of these women is abuse—domestic, emotional, verbal, physical, sexual, or substance abuse, or a combination of them. About 40 percent were sexually abused as a young child. Another common thread is chronic depression. Mental health issues are frequent, adding to the complexity of an already challenging life situation. Chronic health problems affect 75 percent of our women residents—about three times the average for women in their age group. Some have warrants out for their arrest, have had their children in and out of foster home placement, are chemically dependent, or have been involved in prostitution. All struggle to live on incomes below poverty guidelines.

A Ministry of Hospitality

After a year of being the case coordinator for Volunteers of America at CornerStone, our church body called me to specialized ministry to reach out to rural homeless families. I was delighted when they made CornerStone Ministries a church judicatory-authorized worshiping community. Now, I serve the families as both case worker and as pastor. One visualizes ministry with an existing congregation and a church building; this call has neither. The worshiping community is primarily the residents and families who are the present sojourners here.

This is a ministry of hospitality, one of welcoming those who have no place to call "home." Families come when they are being evicted, their housing has been condemned, they are living in their vehicles, their marriage has just broken up, or they are leaving an abusive relationship. Some come from a treatment center or mental health institution. Sometimes CornerStone is the place for moms to be reunited with their children. The furnished apartments are inviting and comfortable, often the nicest place these families ever have lived. I remember a visiting confirmation student that had come with his pastor to learn more about homelessness in their backyard who said, "Wow! This place is nice."

The ministry of hospitality does more than provide housing and food. Each person is given a handmade quilt from the area churches or local quilting group. Hospitality includes acquainting each family with the CornerStone program, staff, and other residents, as well as the local community and its resources. One needs to know where the grocery stores, the hospitals and clinics, the drug store, hardware store, and library are located.

Hospitality includes not just the physical needs of the resident and her children, but also emotional needs. In the past the women may have had concerns about their physical safety, so we may need to work to get an order for protection. CornerStone does not allow perpetrators with a history of abuse on its grounds. Law enforcement is called when necessary. Women gain emotional safety when they are treated with respect and not manipulated or coerced.

A Place for Spiritual Growth

This ministry of hospitality is like a retreat ministry. The quiet, secluded wooded setting on some five hundred acres provides a safe place to sort out one's life. There is a deep sense of the Spirit's working in the lives of the resident and her family. To fully utilize supportive transitional housing, it needs to be a *kairos* time for that individual—a time when one is ready, able, and supported enough to make changes, to move forward toward one's hopes and dreams. The Spirit works growth, which provides readiness to let go of the garbage and old ways of doing life. The CornerStone staff work to remove the obstacles that have prevented women from becoming more self-sufficient.

At the deepest level, the issues with which each woman struggles are spiritual issues. Questions abound. "Is there a good and gracious God? Can things change for me and my family?" There is the hunger for healing and a search for trust, respect, self-worth, and hope. Oftentimes the spiritual questions arise around the kitchen table, from the mouth of a child, or during our weekly educational group meetings. I open with a meditation and a time for reflecting and sharing. We walk through some deep waters as residents share the times they stood tall, were resourceful, met a challenge, or learned a lesson.

While growing up, I thought about being a missionary, but did not see myself being a missionary pastor. CornerStone is a mission field in my backyard. There are some residents with little to no religious resources; others have faith with little or no contact with a church body or congregation; still others have an active faith. Some women hold childhood memories of church, some good and others not so good. There are many opportunities for teaching and for reaching those who live at the edges of society.

Traditionally, congregations have not been very effective at working with high-risk families. It takes special efforts, commitment, and follow-through. Ministry is not a one-time deal. We need to be aware of the obstacles a low-income, single-parent family faces in becoming involved with a congregation. Families, including our CornerStone families, are looking for a church to call home. They need to be welcomed for who they are and with the gifts they bring. They deserve to be supported as they move through a difficult time in their lives.

Each year CornerStone hosts a Homeless Memorial Service near the longest night of the year, a few days before Christmas, to draw the community's attention to homelessness in our state. Residents, former residents, community members, and staff gather to remember and to honor the homeless who have died during the past year. Luminaries line the sidewalk and cluster around the altar. The first year we remembered forty-seven persons, including two young children. Near the close of the service a bell is tolled for those who have died with no earthly home. In addition to the worship service, we have a clothesline filled with garments. Each represents one woman or child who requested housing at CornerStone, but who could not be served. Two years ago we placed 26 new residents; we had inquires from 153 more. Last year we placed 56 new residents, but had 71 inquiries from 237 other women and children. The need for transitional housing far outstrips what is available.

Weaving New Lives

Last fall was the beginning of CornerStone's weaving studio. Each resident has the opportunity to work there, learning each step to produce a finished weaving. This studio was first envisioned as a place to practice work-readiness skills, including getting one's children up, dressed, and to our child care facility so that one can get to "work" at the studio as scheduled, as well as learn the art of weaving.

The results have been amazing and beautiful, both the woven creations and the benefits to the weavers themselves. Betty said, "Weaving has given me something to look forward to." Joan tells, "I have a great sense of pride in my workmanship and now I know I can make something beautiful!" Doing a "hands on," creative activity has helped the women to focus, relieved stress, and given them a sense of accomplishment and ownership. They have learned responsibility—to come, to plan their project, and to follow it through to completion. For Diane, weaving at CornerStone was the first thing she had done without being told she couldn't do it. The transformation in some of the residents has been remarkable.

This summer the weaving studio had its first open house. Each of the more than forty visitors added a strip to make a weaving. A few one-of-a-kind pieces were sold. The women weavers continue to develop products of great beauty, and to search for market outlets. They hope one day this studio will be self-supporting.

Allison has woven a rug she calls "Harvest of Life." The rug itself is stunningly attractive, but it also represents her story, which gives meaning to its beauty. Allison has written: "This rug represents where I was in life and where I am now. Eight years of being trapped in a bad relationship while two children were depending on me, and knowing I had nowhere to go, left me unable to break away. When I finally found the loophole to freedom, my children were taken and placed in foster care and I was homeless. Lots of footwork, moving to CornerStone, and getting my children back have helped me start a new life. A series of tragic events recycled into a new and wonderful life. A collection of discarded material recycled into a beautiful rug."

When Lisa and her four children came, she had a high school diploma but had been out of the workforce for nine years. Lisa's goal was to secure employment that would support her family. First, she was trained as a certified nursing assistant, then as a home health aide. Lisa started working and took classes to be an emergency medical technician. Now she has a job as an EMT. Lisa traded her old car in for a newer model. She says with a huge smile, "This is the first car I have ever owned that didn't have any rust!" Having qualified for a special rural development loan, Lisa has purchased and recently moved into her own home. Step-by-step, Lisa's dreams of self-sufficiency are becoming a reality.

Many residents of CornerStone experience transformation. It is growth. It is new life. It is hope. This is the gospel "with skin on."

CHAPTER SEVENTEEN

Ordinary Interruptions: The Ministry of Presence

Maryann Cox Morgenstern

The winter winds may be fierce, but the land is beautiful. Life is hard and feelings are deep. In the Montana expanse, Maryann's presence is needed. With warmth and joy, she wisely listens as people share their lives. There she discerns her call to ministry.

Ministry is filled with interruptions. God, too, has interrupted our creation by becoming flesh and being born as a child, Jesus. This holy interruption brought healing, hope, and love. People interrupted Jesus' life, and he encountered them in the interruptions. The interruption that made creation groan was Jesus' suffering and death. In the glorious resurrection of Jesus from the dead, God confirms that Jesus' interruption is the sure gift of forgiveness of sins and new life. Ministry comes in many shapes and forms, times and places, with colors and shadows. Ministry is not always predictable—it takes openness to the Spirit to capture opportunities. The following three ministry stories are ways in which I have experienced Christ in the interruptions.

I have come to learn that eastern Montana is not a place where people open their lives easily, but when they do, the depth and power of living life pours out. I was assigned to eastern Montana as a first-year pastor, in a full-time call as a co-pastor with Mark, my spouse. We embraced the opportunity to serve where we were needed and in the place where we were called. Eastern Montana is in the beautiful high plains of the country. Some people hold the romantic view that this area is still filled with cowboys, with tumbleweeds rolling the range, and gunfights in town on Friday nights. Myths do not die easily. The reality is that in this part of the country there are strong families who work hard every day because that is the way life is for them. Ranchers own thousands upon thousands of acres in this wide-open prairie to run cattle and sheep; farmers grow crops that help feed the world. This area of Montana is different from the rest of the state and holds its own wonder, history, and people who are like no other, and yet at the very same time like everyone else.

Aaron's Insistence

I met a very special couple in a very difficult time. Charles and Joyce were married during the fullness of their lives. Joyce was a creative and energetic teacher who had a deep connection with the families of the community. She lived with cancer. The year I met her the cancer was in its final stages. The inevitable was now a reality. Joyce was in Hospice care, which provided support for both her and her family.

Charles still cared for Joyce at home, with frequent visits from Michelle, their daughter, and Aaron, their six-year-old grandson. Charles found concentration at work hard and the many long hours with Joyce sometimes difficult, but he was always supported by friends and family. People stopped at their home to visit, meeting in the living room, which was now Joyce's bedroom. She was in the midst of activity so she was never alone.

Her last days passed quietly and peacefully until her body finally gave out. As one of Charles and Joyce's pastors, I was called to their house after she died. I arrived at the same time as some of the family. After a long day of tears and sadness, Charles knew he had to make the final arrangements. I came back later that evening and discussed the funeral with him. Joyce and Charles had intentionally put together a lot of the plans. It was apparent that they had a good grasp of ritual. They planned important parts of the service that aided healing for the mourners. Michelle was also a part of the discussion, and without skipping a beat, Aaron popped up from the basement. He knew that something important was happening.

Aaron came to the table where father and daughter were engaged in serious conversation. He pulled up a chair, wriggled it alongside his grandfather's and slid a box onto the table. Upon opening the box, he fumbled through the trinkets and cards it contained. Before long, Aaron pulled out a deck of very special cards, closed the box, and dropped it to the floor. Settling down on his knees, he carefully removed the rubber band from the deck of cards and began to lay them out in three even rows and columns.

The finalization of plans was very hard for Charles, yet he seemed to stay above his pain. Aaron, at his side, began to turn the cards over two at a time. Before long Aaron said, "a match," with unreserved excitement. Michelle, shocked at his interruption, tried to quiet her son while her dad and I continued talking. Sheepishly, Aaron turned to his grandpa and said, "Look Grandpa, a bird match. I remember Grandma loved to watch the birds at the feeder." Charles responded with a casual grunt and continued with the funeral planning. Michelle firmly told Aaron to play quietly. He continued to turn over the cards. Then he turned to Charles and said, "It's your turn, Grandpa." This time Charles firmly told his grandson, "Not now Aaron!" I could not help being a little distracted with Aaron's intense focus on playing cards.

Michelle, wanting to keep Aaron quiet, gave in to his plea and took a turn at his game. At Aaron's next turn, he said excitedly again, "A match!" This time his explanation was his memory of Grandma taking him for a walk in the park. He then looked at his grandpa, who was still talking about a reading he wanted to use in the funeral service, and then looked at me. This time, without Aaron's asking, I took a turn at his game, but made no match. Michelle went next. After turning over her first card, which was a cat, Aaron enthusiastically pointed to a card for her to turn over next. She smiled and turned over the card he pointed out, and it was a cat. Anticipating the match, it was obvious Aaron had another story to share, this one about how much Grandma loved cats.

Charles couldn't help being drawn in by Aaron's game and waited to see what card Aaron would turn over next. Aaron's turn proved to be another match and another story. Charles graciously took his turn and offered a story with the first card he turned over about how much Joyce loved needlework. My turn was next; I turned over one card and asked Aaron to share another story.

The game played out, the stories were shared, and the grief-filled funeral plans were wrapped with precious memories. Aaron's persistence in playing the game he needed to play was an interruption that brought the beginning of healing for the rest of us. In God's incredible providence there are interruptions in our lives that we want to ignore, but in truth they may be avenues of hope and healing.

Teenage Tears

Healing does not always come easy and never can start until we wrestle with the source of pain. One evening my daughters and I were out with my horses. After the girls and I groomed them, I watched the girls ride them off into the hills. It was a beautiful evening and quiet until I heard a car rumble over the cattle guard. I turned to watch the car, but could not tell who it was until they pulled up behind the truck and got out. It was Holly and Sarah, two of the youth from church.

I must have had a perplexed look on my face. I had not expected to see them come out to the pasture. Holly was crying.

> *Death is that last interruption that we will all have to face someday.*

I walked over to the girls and Sarah apologetically said, "Sorry we came out here without your knowing, but we just had to talk to you. We didn't know what else to do." The youth had picked up on the fact that I spend what little spare time I have out with my horses. I had given them the freedom to seek me out and they knew where my favorite place was. It amazes me that even in my safest place, openness welcomes others.

I immediately asked, "What's going on?" Through the tears, each taking turns talking when the other could not, I heard the long story of a car accident and their friend being killed. This invasion in their young, tender lives was more than they could deal with. They said their parents were busy trying to find out the details of the accident and had not heard their pain. Holly and Sarah wanted to know if their friend had suffered, was he saved, where was his soul, was he in heaven. The questions went on. There was not enough space for me to answer their questions, even in this wide-open pasture. I knew we were not going to review all the confirmation classes they had had on baptism and being claimed by God through Jesus, who died so that we might have eternal life and the forgiveness of our sins. They had learned those lessons. I knew that I could not be rehearsing for them the full reality of bodily death and that Scripture tells us that the perishable puts on the imperishable, and that we will be changed. Mere words about that mystery would not be heard at this moment. Their tears and hugs reminded me that what might be more important was to hold them and listen to their hearts. I did.

In the quiet of the big Montana expanse, I felt that my presence was what they needed. God provided the rest. I shared tears with them and helped them name their pain. We sat on the tailgate of the truck and watched God's incredible gift of the evening sun and knew that being together was enough for that day. Ministry did not come planned or in the office or by appointment, but it came nonetheless. Through God's grace we cared for one another and experienced God's presence in and with each of us.

Ash Wednesday Death

Death is that last interruption that we all will have to face someday, but it is with Jesus Christ that we will always find the final word. This past winter was not a bad winter as it goes around here. The weather was cold enough and we had our share of snow. Toward the end of the season, in February, we had a big storm that gave us snow that equalled the amount we had had up to that point all winter. One Tuesday the flakes started in heavy, so that by noon the school closed. The buses were sent home just in time. The snow worsened. That night there was no relief and the wind drifted walls of snow everywhere. The next day school was canceled.

It was the beginning of Lent, Ash Wednesday. Mark came in to say he was off to the office, across the street, and that he would make his way to the garage to get the snow shovel and dig a path before I came over. I finished getting ready and within ten minutes the front door flew open and Mark yelled, "Maryann, get some blankets. Frank is down. Hurry!" My heart raced. I grabbed a woolen blanket from the closet and a bright red-print picnic blanket we used in the summer. I ran out the door looking around frantically to see where they were. Frank could have been anywhere around the church because he was the groundskeeper and removed the snow in winter. As I could have guessed, they were right in front of the steps to the office. Frank probably had wanted to clear a path to the office for us this snowy morning. Directly out our front door were Mark and two people kneeling down. I plodded as best I could through the wet, deep, heavy snow. Frank was on the ground and Lisa and Barb, church members who were coming to the church office, were doing CPR.

Mark and I put the woolen blanket on Frank, who still was not responding. The wind seemed fierce by now so I dropped one end of the picnic blanket, handed one side to Mark and we made a windbreak. Within minutes, two men from the police department arrived and took over the CPR. Before long, the ambulance arrived and took Frank to the hospital. Patty, his wife, pulled up to the scene and, after we surrounded her with information and hugs, we followed the ambulance. At the hospital, the team of care professionals were waiting and continued attending Frank.

Some time later a doctor came to tell Patty that Frank had died at the scene, and their attempts to revive him had been unsuccessful. Frank died that snowy Ash Wednesday, outside of church. Not only did the snow paralyze the community, but so did the death of Frank. It was a few days before the streets could be dug out. That was the beginning of a long Lenten season that continually drew me to the cross. God's final interruption of an empty grave is the hope and peace that strengthen me for ministry in all its forms.

There are many ways in which parish ministry is interrupted. It is in knowing that God is ever present and always guiding that I can dare to celebrate the interruptions of ministry.

CHAPTER EIGHTEEN

Ordinary Questions: Parish Health Ministry

Sr. Mary Owen Haggerty, O.P.

An ordinary question: "How come?" Readers are invited to explore such straightforward questions and basic answers with Sr. Mary Owen as she shares her ecumenical opportunities for parish health ministry. She sees her mission field as the community, her mission as health and wholeness in Christ.

How come? How come we who believe in the God of life cannot promote lifestyles of wellness in the parish? How come some people fall through the cracks in a local community, not receiving the heath ministry services they need? How come two Protestant churches hired a Roman Catholic sister to be their parish health minister?

Ten years ago, when I was beginning a move from full-time to part-time ministry within my own Sinsinawa Dominican Order, the parish nurse concept was gaining momentum in north central Iowa. A parish nurse from there spoke at a seminary's rural ministry conference in Dubuque. Among the 150 people in attendance was a Lutheran pastor from northeastern Illinois, the director of Rural Outreach at the Dubuque Mercy Health Center, and me, a semi-retired RN from Wisconsin. The pastor was looking for a parish nurse, the director was looking for someone to take part in her fledgling program, and I was looking for a setting in which to offer what my background and experience in geriatric and psychiatric nursing had brought forth in me. Our collaboration began at that rural ministry conference and that's "How come?"

Ecumenical Ministry Opportunities

Initially, my services were offered two different times to Roman Catholic churches in the area. I thought I was making them an offer they couldn't afford to pass up, but they did. The parish nurse concept was very young and untried in this part of Illinois. The churches I approached maintained elementary schools with all the required expenditures, and even though the stipend I requested was very modest, their budgets would not allow for my joining their staffs. I now look upon these circumstances and what felt like rejection with kindness and thanksgiving. It allowed me to begin my most serious and extended exposure to denominations other than my own—and that's "How come?"

I began in my early sixties to broaden my view of God's actions beyond the world of Roman Catholics. Years ago people may have asked of a Catholic sister serving a Protestant congregation, "Which way will the conversion pendulum swing?" Today such a question is asked only occasionally and by those unfamiliar with the ecumenical climate of East Dubuque, Illinois. I began to notice similarities among the congregations at every turn. Catholics are not the only ones who avoid the front pews, nor are they unique in expecting that the Sunday service will not extend beyond the usual, traditional, and unchangeable time frame. Creedal statements as presented in the *Book of Prayers* are nearly identical; elements of the service and ritual are similar; Holy Communion is deeply reverenced.

These similarities form part of the answer to another question often put to me early on. "Has anyone objected to having you visit or refused your care?" No, never! I suggest that is so primarily because deep down we hold in common many precious beliefs; we show a solid foundation for trusting each other. Second, when one is in need of health-related services of any kind or when one is searching for information, comfort, reassurance, or courage, doctrinal distinctions regarding the dynamics of salvation, the place of Mary in devotions, or the power of the Papacy, seem to have no immediate relevance. Third, nurses, especially those with some maturity, generally enjoy the honor of being trusted quickly.

Extending Healing Ministries

Three years later, as a result of having been involved regularly in local ecumenical meetings with pastors from Grace Lutheran Church, St. Mary's Catholic Church, and Wesley United Methodist Church, and because East Dubuque has a very efficient "grapevine," which informed people of my ministry at Grace, I was offered a position at Wesley. I function there as I do at Grace, providing personal health consultation and referral information, connecting people with resources, encouraging positive health practices, preaching, annointing, praying, laughing, hugging, and occasionally providing shut-ins with a taste of Sinsinawa's homemade pie.

> *Much of what I learned from listening has prepared me to walk with them along their path of decline.*

An opportunity for service, which is not included in the job description, has evolved for me over the past six years that is unique to The United Methodist Church. It has resulted from the characteristic itinerancy of the United Methodist clergy. We have had three pastors in the past six years. I am seen by many as a symbol of continuity, providing a sense of security and connectedness to church. This is particularly significant for long-time members who are no longer able to attend services regularly. My role at the parish level is to encourage the healing ministry in the church, which has very deep roots in the New Testament. I go to services every Sunday and greet people, and rotate staying for the entire service at each congregation throughout the month. When I do, I lead the prayers of the congregation. I am available before the service for consultation, to do blood pressure checks, and sometimes to teach classes on wellness or a health-related topic. I need to know the parish well enough to assess needs.

I visit people in the hospital and health care facilities and in their homes. I like individual health counseling best of all. People may recently have come from a doctor's appointment or from the hospital with a lot of information, some of which they would like to talk over or have interpreted with suggestions for implementation. I see that as my forte. I see a parish health minister as helping people look at their lifestyles and perhaps eliminate detrimental habits. I listen, answer their ordinary questions, and become a liaison between them and common resources.

Ruth and Zac

The importance of continuity has been apparent in the lives of Ruth and Zac. Six years ago when I first met them, both were in reasonably good health. Zac, then eighty-three, was making a good recovery from a fall from the roof of their back porch. Ruth, six years younger, was a cancer survivor, having lived through the rigors of surgery and chemotherapy for ovarian cancer.

Perhaps the most important thing I did for them at that time, since they required no specific nursing procedures, was to focus on getting to know them. So, much of what I learned from listening to their life review, their church experiences, their family relationships, and from watching them interact with each other with humor, displeasure, and anger, has prepared me to walk with them along their path of gradual but persistent decline.

About three years ago Ruth suffered a major stroke that disabled her right side and left her with a severe speech impediment. The level of care she required made a move from their home of forty years to an assisted living facility a necessity. Although we had talked previously about this potential event, the reality was nevertheless a major shock. Zac and I talked repeatedly over the next several months about loss of the treasured space called home, Ruth's loss of the ability to communicate verbally, and their loss of mobility, since Ruth was the driver in the family.

Ruth listened attentively to all these conversations, adding by sign or squeal or grunt her approval or disapproval. Ruth and I began to hold hands a lot, tapping into the very powerful means of communication: touch.

The assisted living apartment into which Ruth and Zac moved served them well for about one and one-half years. They profited from regularly prepared meals, medication supervision, socializing, and proximity to younger family members. However, being the provider of nighttime care for Ruth, which meant helping her to the bathroom two or three times a night, proved to be too much for Zac. He had a series of slight strokes that weakened him considerably. He began to need care also and it became necessary for this courageous couple to be uprooted again. From their three-room apartment home, they reluctantly moved into a new, one-room home in the local nursing care center.

Here is what I think is happening with Ruth and Zac and me:

- We're trying to come to grips with the pain of continual loss.
- We're trying to stay connected with family members, several of whom I also visit.
- We're trying to cooperate with the medical and nursing recommendations.
- We're wondering what God has in store for us; where is God's will?
- We're learning to pray together better. Zac, the non-churchgoer, is quick to remind me if I start to leave without praying.
- We are hanging in there with one another.
- We love one another.

What Difference Does It Make?

Finally, I believe my presence in the East Dubuque churches has served as a catalyst for the broader community. I take special delight when my

Methodist and Lutheran parishioners ask me to stop by to see their Catholic friends. I sometimes serve as "minister-in-the-cracks" to those people who are between churches, because I have become acquainted with them in their time of need. A nurse sees across denominations. I take it as a compliment when someone says, "I'm glad you have an ecumenical spirit." When people ask, "How come you serve both Protestant churches in town?" my quick reply to the question may sound curt: "What difference does it make?" At a deeper level we have come to see it makes a difference in people's lives. It makes a difference in the community.

I cheer when ten to twelve of my Dominican Sisters and coworkers show up for a fund-raising spaghetti dinner or soup supper about which they knew nothing a few years ago. My heart is warmed by hearing the small church choirs sing music I know they learned as part of the large civic chorus at Sinsinawa.

Often I find myself asking "How come?" How come you have been so fortunate to be admitted so fully into the Protestant worshiping community? How come you have been so fortunate to hear and sing the rich music of the Methodist and Lutheran traditions? How come many homes and hearts in East Dubuque and beyond have been opened to you? I find the answer in a prayer that is said often within my religious community:

> Providence can provide
> Providence did provide
> Providence will provide
> Thanks be to God

How come? Why not?

CHAPTER NINETEEN

Ordinary People: Shared Ministry

Kathryn Bielfeldt

Kathy provides a candid account of how she, as a woman who is blind, waited for, and received a call. This is a story of how people in rural St. John's congregation learned to share ministry and then had to learn how to share Kathy. Her story may be unique, but the situation of rural congregations facing the challenge of no longer having "their own" pastor presents a challenge to the entire church. Is a congregation still a congregation if it does not have a pastor to call its own? How do people and churches learn to share ministry?

I waited for a call for eighteen months. That's quite a while, but I was not surprised. I can remember praying for a call, but I never could get an interview. When people heard I was blind they didn't even consider me. The longer I waited, the less confident I became. Then one day I received a phone call. I remember it well. It was the president of St. John's Lutheran Church of Campbell Hill, Illinois.

The bishop had recommended me. He had telephoned the congregation and told them he had a pastoral candidate for them—and that it was a woman. The president paused and then said, "We can handle that." The bishop added, "And she's blind." Again a pause. And then the president said, "Well, why can't we at least look into it?" They wanted to interview me. I knew they were afraid.

When I arrived for the interview, the congregation members were very informed. They were interested and wanted to ask questions, but they were scared to death to ask them. An older pastor who had been serving them for several years started to speak. I worried that he would ask something about having a woman as pastor. But he said, "If someone were to invite you out to dinner after service, I wonder if you would go." After that, the ice was broken.

The first time they voted, all approved except one person. The second vote was unanimous. They hadn't had a pastor of "their own" for several years. They had been yoked with another congregation and were going through a "divorce," so to speak, from that relationship. It seemed important for them to have a pastor. It is not a wealthy congregation. I was called to a half-time position. I have been serving them for nine years, and working, in effect, almost full time.

Learning to Share Ministry

From the very beginning, I tried to make it as clear as possible that we would have to work together so that I could function to capacity. We would need drivers and readers. When I circulated the initial request, twenty drivers and fifteen readers responded. After six weeks, I received two calls from volunteers who just wanted to remind me that they "had not driven yet and were ready." Soon the regular attendance in this 110-member church was 70. At the first communion service, I asked the people to identify themselves at the table by name so that I could personalize their receiving the elements. Everything quickly seemed to fall into place.

The church secretary, Barb, works just part time, but she does a lot. Once a week we go through the worship materials so that I can put the service into Braille. Then she reads the mail to me and we work out some of the financial matters. If we have funerals or weddings, she works extra so we can put the services together. We're partners and friends too. Barb says she's done things together with her pastor she never thought she could do. She's even helped me to take my dog, Zephaniah, to the vet. I sometimes worry about having someone replace her when she retires, but I think we could handle that too.

The people who drive me to pastoral calls have developed a sensitivity to ministry. They know when to go in and when to wait in the car. Most often they visit the people with me; we all have something to contribute. Then we share communion. I have learned a lot through them about the people in the community.

These are ordinary people. Open country congregations often have special "location" names. St. John's is known as Post Oak. When I first came, the people often modestly described themselves as being "just plain old people here." Now they are all ears. They want to grow. They knew they had to or there wouldn't be a congregation here. We've talked about the importance of people using their talents and how we are all ministers of Jesus Christ. They have begun to claim those gifts and develop confidence in their ministry skills. I would hope they continue to use them whether or not I'm their pastor. We've learned to share ministry.

It's the Simple Things

I'll always remember the time a gentleman was dying of cancer. When he first found out, he and his wife came to my home to tell me about it. He wasn't expected to live much longer. I visited them in their home almost every week. Finally he went into the hospital. I remember the last day I saw him—the day before he died. He had not been responding to much. I love to sing in my ministry, so I

> *They have to learn how to talk my language and I have to learn how to talk theirs.*

went to his side and started to sing "How Great Thou Art." He began making sounds; he was singing too. After I stopped, he seemed at peace. Just a few hours later he died. It was also touching for those who had come to be there with me. In sharing in this ministry, we are all learning about death.

There have been some funny moments, too. One day when Barb and I were going to make a hospital call in a nearby city, it was raining very hard. We were having a difficult time finding a parking place. Barb thought I could just get out and go in and she would pick me up after the visit. I asked her, "Where's the hospital door?"

She responded, "Just get out and walk straight ahead and you'll walk straight into the doors."

I did get out and walked straight ahead—straight in the direction I had exited the car. She had meant straight ahead *of* the car! I didn't have an umbrella, but I kept on walking straight, and was getting pretty wet. Finally she called to me, "I forgot to tell you to turn left." We've laughed a lot about that. They have to learn how to talk my language and I have to learn how to talk theirs.

It's the simple things.

I came here with my guide dog, Zephaniah. He's almost twelve years old; we've been together for ten of those years. In the congregation in Michigan where I did my student internship, he could process down the aisle with me. But the church here at Post Oak is smaller and there's not much room in the chancel. I've learned to move around in this setting very well, because it's become so familiar. The people walk in and out of the church with me—so I can walk a straight line. The children serving as acolytes have learned to work with me in the worship area.

The children and I have learned to work together in confirmation class too. The young people are wonderful; I don't have problems with discipline. We hold the confirmation classes in my home; it's not that large a class. Sometimes we have a meal together. The parents take turns fixing the food and then we have class.

One child liked to kid; he was lots of fun. In order to get ready for the class, I would have to set certain chairs out around the table. After class was over, the youth learned how to put their chairs away. One night I was looking for one of my chairs. I wondered if any of the kids had played a trick on me and put it on the top of the table, but I felt and it wasn't there. So I had to call Barb, of all things, to help me find my chair. Turned out it was simply in the middle of the room. Who would have thought the secretary would have to help her pastor find her chair?

It's the little things that pose problems, not the large challenges. I receive much Braille material, which I need. But it takes up so much space, I don't know where to put it anymore. I'm hoping I someday can purchase a computer that talks, but that would pose yet another challenge—I would need to find the time to learn to use it effectively!

A New Challenge

The people of Post Oak are proud and excited that I'm their pastor, and part of their family. Like families do, sometimes they've given me a surprise party. The relationship has been very positive, but even acceptance can also have its problems. In some ways they feel they own me, and now we face a new challenge.

The bishop called me the summer before last. Would I be interested in working together with another area pastor to serve two neighboring congregations who didn't have pastors? The bishop said it would be a year before anything could develop, in order to give people time to think about it. But things came together sooner than expected, and about a month later I was sharing ministry beyond my own congregation. The people of St. John's didn't have time to get prepared; it was hard on me too. The people weren't upset with me, or the other two congregations; they were mostly upset with the bishop. We had a lot of things to line up quickly, especially drivers. One congregation is twenty miles away; the other only ten. The people come and pick me up and then bring me home again. St. Peter's congregation is in open country and known as Wine Hill. Peace, Chester, is in town, so it has no "location" name.

The other pastor would take a month at one congregation (plus his own) and I would take the other, plus my own. I'm excited about serving the two other congregations, although rotating month by month is difficult. I'm not considered the full-time, permanent pastor of either church, and in fact, I am classified as a part-time pastor on a contractual basis.

Peace congregation had lost three-quarters of their members, which created all sorts of problems. I had not known things were so bad. I grew upset about it and really prayed, wondering if I could handle it. Their annual meetings used to be three and one-half hours long and members were constantly at one another's throats. Now the meetings conclude in just one and one-half hours and they are more peaceful. One woman who had been taking a central leadership role began to include me. That cooperation seemed to rub off on others and spark a new dedication. Truthfully, at the moment, Peace has been the more exciting and wonderful for me because of the challenges I was given; the place that circumstances indicated would be the less satisfying has proved to be the more satisfying.

St. John's has been wonderful in learning to share ministry. Now I know this one setting is not the only one where I could ever serve. I have liked being here all these years. I love them dearly and they love me, but someday they might need someone else to serve them, so they don't get into a rut. It's reassuring to know now that I have mobility.

Rural Congregations and Loss

Most of the people have accepted sharing their pastor, but some worry about the money aspect. They wonder if they are receiving their fair share of my work. Rural congregations struggle with many losses: the local school, farm income, population. When do they lose their identity? We as a church body are working to help several congregations, especially smaller ones, move toward sharing ministry in a cluster. Even though the congregations aren't too happy about it, they know they must.

Their identity resides not simply in their pastor, although having a pastor is a sign of independence. It's a matter of fearing they will lose who they are. A similar situation arose in the round of school consolidations. Even though communities gained some educational benefits, they lost identity. Is the request to share ministry a sign that they will soon no longer exist? The trauma is real. Things become different for both parties when we share, but we are trying. Only God knows how it's going to turn out.

147

God certainly works in mysterious ways, but it's all been a gift. That doesn't mean it's always been easy, but all is a gift! I've grown a lot and I hope the people I've worked with have too. I think we have all benefited from knowing our help comes from the Lord, and from one another.

PART FOUR
NURTURING COMMUNITY

The Church is not just the vessel that bears the good news of Jesus Christ; the Church is good news. It is gospel action. We are called to nurture community, caring for people in the name of Christ as we bear Christ to the world. Churches sometimes get in the way of such witness; they may seemingly stifle any good news or stand in the way of justice ministry. But the Church is what we have. It is the Body of Christ, holy, Spirit-filled; it is also a collection of human beings who bicker and balk. Just as individual Christians need daily to remember their baptism, so too leaders need to nurture community by reminding people, through Word and sacraments, that they are a beloved, forgiven body in whom the Spirit dwells. Then the Church becomes not so much burden or claim as gift.

We are called to nurture community through a ministry of leadership. Sometimes we will need to critique the activity—or inactivity—of a church. Sometimes we simply give thanks for faithful members ministering in the world. But more important than our attitudes or actions is belief, not in the structures we create, but in the fact that this group of people, always inadequate, in some out-of-the-way place, is the Body of Christ. Such belief is a challenge in itself. Likewise, members may have a hard time believing our leadership is Spirit-led. Even, maybe especially, at such times when we are most disillusioned, the Spirit breathes new life into this Body. Then we are called once again to nurture the Church to be what it already is in Christ Jesus.

In nurturing community, we participate in God's mission. It is not that the Church has its own mission, but rather the mission of God includes the Church, and creates Church as it goes. As we lead a people to know God's will and minister faithfully in Christ's service, Christ will be strengthening this body. It becomes a living, breathing organism, and grows accordingly.

The people whom we are privileged to lead are part of a larger body, the Church both historic and global. In Part Four we travel from West to Midwest, from East Coast to the South. We move from urban to rural and back again to the city. We view the church at work from a kitchen, from the streets, and even from the air, trying to gain perspective. Often we become overly engrossed in our little corner of the world, enmeshed in our issues, or desperate to save this congregation. Just when we begin to believe this congregation of problematic people is not the church anymore, we are called once again to trust God, to liberate Christians and to live our vocations. In so doing, we will nurture community.

We begin in Denver with Karen Weissenbuehler. If the Body of Christ is to grow, the whole congregation needs to be nurtured. Ministerial leadership requires vision, and, just as important, the ability to help people love and learn from one another. This can take years of faithful, caring nurture. How slowly or quickly does one need to go? How much diversity, in age and economic class as well as race, can a community tolerate? How can we help people move beyond mere toleration to celebrate diversity? How do we believe God is leading this congregation into God's promised future? This urban congregation, founded shortly after World War II is now in a changing neighborhood. Christ's face appears in surprising places and hues. Karen tells of nurturing community through a ministry of redevelopment.

Christine Iverson, called to full-time disaster response work, frequently also serves as interim pastor in congregations in transition. There she often has discovered congregations steeped in conflict. How do you believe a congregation mired in conflict is God's holy church? How do you nurture a community that has learned patterns of distrust and unhealthy ways of coping with differences? Dealing with diversity is not just an urban challenge. In rural areas more differences among people emerge than might at first appear. Christine's leadership role was to create a safe place to be different together. She used her authority first to disallow unhealthy "anonymous" behaviors. Then she and the congregation could create new patterns for trusting life together. Such nurture takes time, and she as pastor knew she needed ongoing nurture herself to sustain her for the duration. Ministry among congregations in conflict in many ways resembles ministry during and in the aftermath of disaster.

Across the continent, in metropolitan New York, diversity—not just ecumenical but interfaith—is a daily reality. Kimberly Wilson effectively uses the ministry of education to nurture community, and not merely within her church's own walls. Through her personal friendship with a rabbi, the two work together for authentic exchange and cooperation in a pluralistic, public world. How do we participate in Christ's mission, not using a fortress mentality, but by more fully claiming our identity in relationship? How can one engage in ecumenical and interfaith education, not just by "borrowing," or learning "about," but by learning from and with one another? Through educational ministry the community grew, not just in numbers but in depth. In Kim's story we see risky, joyful, caring, celebrative nurture of two congregations and the community beyond.

Alicia Anderson is a campus minister. She describes nurture not in her office, or in a classroom, but in a kitchen. That's where women for centuries were supposed to be, of course, but opportunities to lead communities of faith have led them into places of public ministry and higher education. She does not *return* to the kitchen, to the private sphere, but redefines the kitchen as a place large enough for communal activity. In cooking together, people shared new roles. How do we nurture community with eyes diverted just enough to allow people to talk about private fears? Alicia shows how we can give individual attention in the midst of a crowd. She nurtures community through people preparing to feed one another. In our contexts, how might we, non-directively, minister to hurting people? What settings would be conducive to nurture people to nurture each other? By nurturing individuals in the midst of community, we minister believing that we are the Body of Christ and are, individually, members of it.

When I called Bishop Andrea DeGroot-Nesdahl to invite her to write a chapter for this book, she was at home, in her kitchen, canning pears. That's not the story, although it becomes part of her story. She offers three images, including the pears; three vantage points for the ministry of oversight. How do we imagine our work of leadership? Andrea shares her own inner fears, and the choices one has to make in the face of fear. Whatever our calling, our place in church structure, we struggle with the drive to be super-responsible. In the midst of busy schedules, how does one gain perspective? By literally flying above it all, Andrea is able to focus both on the specific needs of local congregations and on the larger image of the Church. Congregations are connected to one another even when they cannot see it; they need to believe the Church is both local and universal. Andrea's ministry as bishop calls her deeply into the life of individual congregations across the state of South Dakota. She faithfully helps them face their struggles and see themselves in relation to the whole church.

We conclude this book—this journey of seeing the church in ordinary places—outside on the streets. Private grief becomes public news. The church is never to be merely a place of private respite secluded from the world. The church was not instituted to save only those within, but to perform a work of service for all humanity. Ann Helmke's ministry as "animating director" of peaceCENTER in San Antonio calls her to challenging, even dangerous, places. Where does one start when the problems are so large? In the Church's call to be a change-agent for peace with justice, we are called out beyond the stories in this book to envision the broad scope of what nurture means. But Ann's story is really quite simple; it's about ordinary prayer. Every context has its dangers. Each local church is challenged to ministry beyond itself, and each minister is called to prayer. Through prayer we are summoned to carry a message of hope and life beyond fear, a gospel meant for community or that will call a new community into being. Come outside and pray.

CHAPTER TWENTY

Ordinary Hope: Ministry of Redevelopment

Karen Weissenbuehler

Where do we find hope for a congregation on the verge of closing its church doors? Whether they are located on the outer edge of an inner city, or at the convergence of suburban and country living, nurturing congregations in transition requires care and perseverance for ministers. Facing diminishing attendance is depressing. Equally challenging is the question, "When new life emerges, how do long-time members deal with the change resulting from growth?"

The early years of Good Shepherd's life, which began fifty years ago, had been marked by an explosion of families and children and optimism. Fifteen years later, the exodus from the church, as well as the neighborhood, began. By 1994, the bleeding that resulted had diminished the congregation to a few die-hard souls on the outer edge of the inner city of Denver, Colorado. Another story of a congregation threatened by extinction!

I was being interviewed as a pastoral candidate who might be capable and willing to help Good Shepherd grow again, both in numbers and vitality. At the second interview with the call committee, someone asked if I had any questions.

"Where do you see hope?" I asked.

Janet answered, "There is a little boy who comes to church here at Good Shepherd on Sundays from time to time. He sits by himself in the back of the church through the service. Sometimes he will play around on the piano afterward. We don't know his last name, or who his parents are, or where he lives. He says his name is "Future.""

At that point Janelle looked around to other members of the call committee and with a smile and a twinkle in her eye said, "We think he's Jesus."

> There's a little boy here who says his name is "Future."

It was a profound moment. The interview proceeded, but no other questions were needed. I had made up my mind. Possibility is born when we are able to see Jesus in the eyes of children and strangers, and especially when a child's name is "Future"! If Good Shepherd could see "Future" in their midst, they would also be people able to hope, able to envision a future, and they would work to make that vision a reality. I accepted the call and began my ministry there a few weeks later.

The boy, Future, returned to Good Shepherd a few times after I began my ministry there in 1994. He sat by himself near the back of the church, and did not engage in conversation. Then he stopped coming and was only occasionally spotted on the street by someone who lived in the neighborhood.

Future, a small African American boy of about nine years of age, was tucked away in my memory for a time as ministry began at this small congregation. Eventually, however, I shared the impact of that interview and of his presence in a sermon I preached to the congregation.

Afterward, Jill, the director of the child care center, said to me, "Pastor, I just learned the other day that Future is in prison.

"Why?" I asked.

She shrugged as she said, "I don't know. It could be truancy, or drug use, or thievery. Maybe he was involved in a gang. I was not able to find out."

Future as a Metaphor

Metaphors are essential for us when we seek direction for doing ministry. Future became more than a little boy to me as time went on. His name became a metaphor for the work that God had for Good Shepherd in this time and place. He represented hope and direction.

God's purpose for a congregation like Good Shepherd is not always clear. When people grow old and die, or move away, when numbers decrease, a sense of hope and of future can be lost. Folks may continue to work hard through those discouraging times, trying to bring life back into a dying body of believers, but a feeling still may dominate, and the result may be further decline.

Then someone notices a sign, like Future, something that at first appearance is just a little boy coming in off the street and sitting through a worship service with the gray-haired few who are gathered.

Then the sign may become a sign of hope, a God-sign saying "Don't get discouraged. See the child. See the future in his face. See that and know that I have a mission for you. Turn your eyes toward me and watch and wait. See what children I will bring to your door."

Things began to take different shape when we began to look at the future with an eye to what God may be doing. We noticed that children were beginning to come to Sunday school and church. Their mothers and fathers came too. Good Shepherd delighted in the new life. New life also brings new challenges.

When Good Shepherd invited a neighboring child care center to move into Good Shepherd's facility about ten years ago, it seemed such a good idea. The center had been previously housed in a nearby church. The move was necessary because that congregation was leaving the neighborhood. The decision to bring the center to Good Shepherd had to be made quickly, and God's future came into Good Shepherd rushing and stomping, with little time for deliberation on our part!

Understandably, because it happened so quickly, there had not been adequate time for the congregation to have needed conversation, so the welcome was a rather hesitant one. Indeed, there was considerable fear and apprehension among Good Shepherd members.

They had been generous with the use of the building in former years, and had experienced the hard realization that outside groups sometimes stole from them. As a result, they had placed locks on most of the cabinet drawers and doors in the kitchen, and regular inventory was taken. Would this group be like the others?

The facility was forty years old and had begun to show its age, though it was kept immaculate. Could it stand the beating that forty-five small children would give it day after day?

A quiet facility became full of sounds—sounds of children playing and crying, sounds of staff restoring order with loud voices. No longer was the fellowship hall accessible at all times. Many felt a loss of control, and were sad over the loss and change. They watched, and waited.

The child care staff saw the response of the church and it made them feel unwanted, untrusted, unappreciated. They did not feel at home. Was this going to work?

Gradually, under the guidance of the pastor at that time, the situation began to change. An intern pastor helped the child care staff reorganize their finances. A few members of the child care center began to work on building good relationships with the church, and a mission statement was created by the child care staff.

The transformation had begun by the time I arrived as pastor at the church. I attempted to build on that transformation.

I remembered my mother's advice: "Always put the best possible construction on what someone says or does." I tried to do that, both with church folks and with child care folks. I remarked whenever possible how I felt that God was working among us to provide good, loving care to the little ones in the center, and what an important ministry this was for our church.

We continued a twice-weekly chapel time for the children, which had begun before I came, and we talked about it among members of the congregation. We invited child care families to special Sundays where child care children participated in a special way in worship. We provided ways in which members could interact on a one-on-one basis with the children.

Then the child care director and her son began to come to worship. So did the assistant director and her daughter. They joined the church and the children were baptized. At long last, the child care center became a part of the Good Shepherd family. We worshiped together and began to converse together. Walls began to fall.

Then a real miracle happened. One night at council meeting someone asked why we had all those locks on the cupboard doors in the kitchen. Someone else made the motion that we remove them. No discussion. The motion carried! Locks were gone within the week! The beginning of a new future began. The child care center was increasingly seen as a great ministry outreach in the neighborhood because of the fantastic, loving care it provided to lots of children.

And the child care center staff finally understands that nearly all Good Shepherd folks are behind them, especially when Good Shepherd had their kitchen renovated. Oh, the renovation was not just for the child care center; the church would benefit as well. But the fear that the building might not pass state codes provided an impetus. After all, the old kitchen was falling apart—the sink was sinking and the stove could not be used. So when the plea went out, the money came in from all sorts of places: other congregations, visitors to worship, fund-raisers, church members. Everyone worked together. The kitchen was dedicated within a year of the first dream and it was paid for in full at that time.

No one can suggest to me that God doesn't work in some pretty spectacular ways, or should I say small, spectacular ways. Of course, it may all have happened without that little boy Future being a part of our church for a while. Maybe we would have found another metaphor. Or maybe we would not have needed a metaphor. But when I look at the children in our child care center, and our growing congregation, I cannot help being thankful for God pulling us into the future by means of a small boy named Future.

Where Is Future Now?

Jill found out where Future lives; it's in a house just down the block from Good Shepherd.

I spotted someone sitting on the front porch one day so I stopped. It was indeed Future's home, and his dad and his dad's uncle were there. I introduced myself and told my story about Future.

"Is Future around?" I asked.

"No," his father replied sadly. "He's in a group home. He's been in a lot of trouble lately—got in with a bad crowd."

Future's dad showed me a picture of Future with a basketball, and another with Future sitting on the lap of Danny Schayes, a former Denver Nuggets star. "Don't know what went wrong," he said quietly. "He was such a good kid."

The ending to this story has yet to be told. I have to believe that Future has a future in God's plan. So does Good Shepherd.

Recently Jill told me she had finally found out what Future's last name is.

"What is it?" I asked.

"You aren't going to believe this," Jill responded. "His last name is Hope."

CHAPTER TWENTY-ONE

Ordinary Safety: Ministry in Conflict and Crisis

Christine E. Iverson

No congregation is free of conflict. The question becomes How do we nurture a community so members can begin to trust one another enough to develop ways of dealing creatively with conflict? How do we proceed to help a congregation become more healthy? Christine Iverson, who frequently serves as an interim pastor, together with leaders in congregations, moved carefully through difficult times, and emerged to claim their mission potential.

"Please God, don't let this be a disaster," was my prayer as I began my first interim ministry. Clearly the congregation was in crisis, but the bishop had confidence in me in spite of my inexperience. I worried through that first interim, praying that crisis would not turn into disaster. I was sure that disaster and parish ministry had nothing to do with each other. Having served in several congregations, including intentional interim ministries and in emergency disaster response, I am convinced that there are helpful parallels between these two ministries.

There is always a level of grief and crisis to an interim position; something has happened that has changed the status quo. Conflict in the congregation, pastoral misconduct, involuntary removal, or loss of membership add levels of shock, grief and fear to the change. Just as in natural disasters, the more severe the trauma, the longer it will take the community to move through the cycles to recovery. Anger, blaming, fear, inability to move forward, denial, and impatience are all a part of the grief. As in a disaster situation, everyday events or comments can trigger fears and hypervigilance leading to a feeling of resurfacing crisis. It helps both pastor and congregation to know that these are common occurrences, they lessen as time goes on, and they aren't automatically a sign that the community is back in disaster. Losing a sense of confidence and security creates the need for reassurance and safe boundaries. Mistrust of one another, hostility, and patterns of disfunction can intensify people's need either to withdraw or seek a rescuer.

A Congregation in Conflict

At one such point, I was called into a neighboring congregation to serve as an intentional interim pastor. There was a lot of conflict in the congregation: mistrust of one another, hostility, and, as I would learn, a decades-long pattern of dysfunction. The congregation had some very real strengths and very gifted people, but was unable to function as community. Beyond the current conflict, a historical pattern pointed to larger systemic issues. Over the months, many symptoms would appear, but the basic issue was one of learning how to be the Body of Christ in community with one another. Unity in Christ was understood in this place as agreement not just on basic matters of faith, but in opinion and practice. The most vocal members had marginalized, scapegoated, and eventually ousted those who did not comply. People were afraid to disagree publicly, which led to secret meetings and anonymous communications. False unity on the surface magnified the dishonesty and lack of trust, producing an atmosphere of division. Disfavor, disagreement, or anger was expressed in terms of "those people," "some people," or "them." The congregation needed to become a safe place for people to explore their individual gifts as God's children and to live out their communal identity at Christ's table.

My calling in the midst of this was to preach and teach the gospel and to care for everyone. My job was not to fix or take ownership of their problems; in fact, I had to take great care not to get coopted by people who saw themselves on opposing sides. As Edwin Friedman wrote:

> We can only change a relationship to which we belong. Therefore, the way to bring change to the relationship of two others . . . is to try to maintain a well-defined relationship with each, . . . to avoid the responsibility for their relationship with one another . . . [and] maintain a "nonanxious presence in a triangle, [since] such a stance has the potential to modify the anxiety in the others."[1]

I was called into relationship with these people and grew to love them through Christ, but I also had to keep clearly before them and myself that I was their interim pastor and this was their congregation. They needed to own their own problems and their own recovery. My task was often to defuse the crises by refusing to take ownership, and then to reframe the "problem" while giving it back to them and asking what they thought could be done.

My role became one of advice and support to everyone. Often people were surprised to see me speaking on the street or at the church with someone they saw as "the opposition," or with someone whom they knew was antagonistic toward me. Although I didn't purposely arrange it that way, I felt it was an important witness that I held the congregation as a body united in Christ even when they did not. God's saving grace was all that would sustain us through this interim period. I, and everyone concerned, would make mistakes and did; that was a given. Especially in rural settings, those mistakes quickly become public knowledge. What was important was living and learning about repentance, reconciliation, and forgiveness.

Support for the Pastor

I found out early in ministry that I can neither sustain my gospel preaching and "nonanxious presence" on my own, nor without regular maintenance. The care and feeding of my own spiritual life are central to keeping myself grounded in grace. Whether I am putting in tremendous hours in the parish or in the aftermath of disaster, I have found that Martin Luther was right: the more stress I have around me, the stronger my prayer and Bible-study life have to be. This is central in my preparation for solid and honest preaching, for serving the community to which I'm called, and for self and family care.

I also have found it critical to build a network of feedback and support for myself outside of a congregation in conflict. I keep in touch regularly with the bishop's assistant, checking the congruence of messages that we are both receiving, and seeking wisdom. Several times, I have sought out a colleague and friend with extensive interim experience and training for advice and support. Supervision from a pastoral counselor/psychologist becomes an extremely important, confidential, and safe way for me to check reality. There I can reveal my anxiety without burdening my personal relationships (carrying it home) or taking it inappropriately back into the congregation. Self-care means that I have to set boundaries around my time and energies, and be intentional about nutrition and rest.

My initial goal is that congregation members encounter stability, whether we are meeting one-on-one, as a small group, in congregational meetings, or in public worship. I try very hard not to explain myself in several ways to different people. The written word in the congregational newsletter also must focus the issues in a clear and public way. The congruity of presence and a person grounded in faith, ethics, and honesty is reassuring to others and helpful to me as well. Clarity is important and is not easy in the midst of conflict.

Clear Boundaries to Provide Safety

Although it sounds contradictory, clear boundaries have to be set so that communication can be open and honest. Those boundaries have to be clarified and repeated again and again. Anonymity and confidentiality are not one and the same. Confidentiality has long been a core value of the Church in confession and in matters of pastoral care, but it does not extend to anonymous communication in any form.

Anonymous communications can be a symptom of dysfunction. In one congregation, members commonly called up the church secretary and left anonymous messages and opinions for "the pastor." Over the years there have been anonymous notes left on my desk, unsigned letters in the mail, unsigned notes to council members, and unidentified phone messages. It took me years to learn that the best way to handle these was not to listen to them or read them, and certainly not to pass them on. Neither is it anyone else's job to be a conduit. The best response is to make clear my openness to criticism and comments in whatever form with any identified person. Not accepting anonymous messages allows me honestly to express lack of knowledge until people face me with their concerns themselves. I also know it is much more destructive for my peace of mind (and congregational unity) to read these messages and try to figure out who is behind them; that only magnifies the atmosphere of mistrust.

The greater the amount of existing conflict and dysfunction, the greater the likelihood that the level of discomfort will rise with this insistence on attaching names and faces to opinions and comments. During one interim, someone asked for a suggestion box so anonymous ideas could be submitted more easily, while at another congregation, there was a request to bring the existing box back into

> There is no way to offer pastoral care, define problems, or work on reconciliation among anonymous people.

use. People claim to be "afraid" of being known as disagreeing, or "afraid" of talking to the pastor. There is no way to offer pastoral care, define problems, or work on reconciliation among anonymous people.

At the same time, congregations are right; their fears need to be taken into account. There needs to be a safe way for people to share their concerns and opinions with their pastor, the council, and with each other. First of all, each meeting needs to begin with the Word and with prayer. Then, boundaries need to be set and maintained:

- The conversation needs to be open, honest, and safe. Honesty is not an excuse for attacking others.
- Speak only for yourself. Others must offer their own opinions and stories.
- This is a "no dumping zone." Sharing is welcome; emotional overload is not.
- There are no dumb questions.
- Everyone has the right to speak. Make room for everyone.
- We are not here to judge, but to listen. Forgiveness and tolerance are imperative for ourselves and for one another.

One Congregation's Turning Point

The turning point for one council came about halfway into the interim. Members raised a congregational issue that had to be dealt with by the council. It was not the bishop's job to settle the dispute, although he was informed. This created a crisis and opportunity for the council in several key areas. First of all, in an atmosphere where reports of council decisions and individual opinions were running wild through the grapevine less than twelve hours after a meeting, council members had to face issues of confidentiality. Second, the council had to take an active role in following through their responsibility outlined in Matthew 18:15-17, by picking representatives to meet with both parties. In doing that, the council had to openly face their own internal disagreements and yet work together in unity through the process. Most important, they were called on to act as the elders of this faith community in a spiritual way, in order to pray and live the gospel in the midst of named people and their pain. This was the beginning of a spiritual change that became the light shining the way for the whole congregation.

Disaster response works best for everyone when there is unity and cooperation. Communal decision-making provides safeguards, calls us each into account, and accomplishes more than one person or agency could do alone. The issue of responsibility for decision-making in committees, council, and in congregational meetings has been one of the most valuable transfers from disaster to congregation. If something is to be done in the name of the congregation, then the congregation or a properly constituted committee needs to make that decision and take responsibility for the consequences.

"Working within the system" will be perceived by some as authoritarian shutdown at first and as a barrier to the mission *they* want to do. In actuality, such communal decisions will protect both the congregation and the individual volunteers. Previously anxious members will begin to experience less fear that an individual or a small group will do something outlandish or against the congregation's will. Volunteers can act with less fear because they will not be abandoned if something goes wrong. On the other hand, discomfort may increase on other levels. It will be more difficult to scapegoat an individual; the demand for open communication and communal involvement will intensify.

One unacknowledged cause of stress in an interim is often the diversity of the congregation. Although the self-image of the congregation (and often the denomination) is of a settled faith community, we are no longer a homogeneous body. Nowadays, many new members are baby boomers with no church experience since childhood; many come from other denominations or have no prior church or faith background. People hold fewer shared values than they realize; they work under different assumptions about what is appropriate to put in the library or serve at receptions. Any congregation has greater mission potential if it can move beyond its fear of difference, which some interpret as "chaos." Healthy diversity can help us break out of patterns of self-destruction or of accepting only those people that "fit."

Policies to Guide

The fear of diversity literally can shut a congregation down. An effective way to calm such fears is proactive—to set safe boundaries and intentionalize communal values by making clear congregational policies. We began in one congregation by seeking out and looking at any old policies that we could find. As in most congregations, policies set at prior meetings were often soon lost and forgotten. We agreed to meet for a day-long retreat to work at setting policies for the congregation.

We used as the groundwork for this process John Carver's method of governance: "The Board's challenge is to be reasonably certain nothing goes awry and at the same time to grant as much unimpeded latitude as possible to those persons with the skill and talent to get the work done."[2] To "make the case for freedom through limits," we talked through some of the difficult situations we had encountered as a council. The goal is to set limits—standards of ethics and prudence. With policies in place, ministry can happen freely, as long as members follow the guidelines. Policies are not constitutional amendments; they can be much more fluid and responsive to changing needs of the congregation. Good policies are as broad as possible, becoming specific only in those areas that require more oversight (such as money and sexual harassment). The council brought policies to the congregation for ratification.

The first policy itself concerned "policies." It outlined the executive council responsibilities, annual review, and current publications to keep members informed. The second stated, "For the sake of unity, the congregation will follow the policies set by the council as set by the constitution." The third policy outlined yearly orientation on policies and procedures, the constitution, and job descriptions. The fourth formalized an unwritten policy that had been verbalized to me before I began my ministry: inclusive language will be used in worship and publications.

After getting their feet wet, the council worked on policy areas that were more difficult, addressing previous issues of disagreement or conflict. Although council members continued to disagree, they developed enough trust to be honest with one another and honor the commitment to keep working together. After this day of retreat and hard work (and laughter and a shared meal), the council continued to work on policies over the coming months, setting another day of retreat for this purpose later that summer. Within a year, the council set forth sixteen policies in the areas of governance, pastor and staff, committees and ministry of the laity, and mission.

This all sounds very procedural and regulatory, but the purpose of these efforts was to reenforce the ministry of the congregation as community in Christ while insuring the safety of its members to act. These policies formed the "on paper" version of the relational faith life to which we are called in baptism. The focus of our life together was not on policies and procedures, but on our identity as the baptized and forgiven children of God, our relationship around Christ's table, and with God. These were merely tools to help build and empower the community.

No matter the conflict or length of interim, the central focus of our ministry together has always been those gifts received through grace: faith, forgiveness, the Word, identity as God's children, the sacraments, and the call to witness and ministry. In their gracefulness, these congregations and members have taught me a great deal about my own faith, spirituality, and leadership as a pastor; they forgave me as I learned with them. To the extent that this happened at all, it is clearly a sign of God's grace.

Notes

1. Edwin H. Friedman, *Generation to Generation: Family Process in Church and Synagogue* (New York: The Guilford Press, 1985), p. 39.

2. This statement is adapted from *Boards That Make a Difference: A New Design for Leadership in Nonprofit and Public Organizations,* 2nd ed., by John Carver (San Francisco: Jossey-Bass, 1997), p. 82.

CHAPTER TWENTY-TWO

Ordinary Friendship: The Ministry of Education

Kimberly A. Wilson

To minister with integrity requires mutual respect and genuine affection for those within the faith community and also one's neighbors. Kim possesses such gracious qualities of leadership. Some look to camaraderie only as a way to escape the demands of leading a congregation. Some leaders engage other professionals merely competitively. How does friendship grow so that it enriches community?

My friend and colleague Rabbi Jo David leaned across the table to me and said quite seriously, "You know we could both be burned at the stake for this." I laughed, a little nervously, I must admit. She was referring to the new liturgy we had created, a Christian ritual that celebrates the Jewish roots of Jesus' Last Supper. We called it our *first* "Last Supper," and we sincerely hoped it wouldn't be our last!

Caught up in a growing trend of congregations wishing to celebrate Passover, my congregation, on Long Island, New York, had asked me if we could reenact Jesus' Last Supper in the context of the Jewish Seder ritual. Our semi-urban context is multicultural and religiously pluralistic. The community is about half Jewish and half Christian, with a smattering of other faiths as well: Hinduism, Buddhism, and Islam to name just a few. Learning to articulate one's own faith clearly while respecting and understanding the faiths of others is essential for ministry in this setting.

As a pastor, I wanted to honor my congregation members' desire to learn more about the Jewish roots of Jesus' institution of the Lord's Supper.

However, I knew that celebrating a Jewish holiday without respecting the integrity and development of Jewish tradition apart from Christianity was problematic. Not only would such a celebration be religiously inaccurate, it would almost certainly prove spiritually offensive to our Jewish neighbors and friends. Knowing that I was treading on rocky religious ground, I turned to my friend and colleague, Rabbi Jo David, for help. As the spiritual leader of a neighboring Long Island synagogue, Union Reform Temple, Jo was happy to help me and my congregation sort out the issues and even co-plan and co-lead an appropriate celebration.

Creating a Common Meal

The problem was how to create a meal consistent with the Passover tradition of Jesus' day while interpreting it so it could be understood by Christians who had not grown up with the Seder tradition. Our solution was to write a new liturgy, which would become a Christian ritual experience and a learning experience for both Christians and Jews. This liturgy came out of our dialogue as we conversed with each other about our own faith traditions. Creating the liturgy was a creative process. As women in ministry, we learned from each other and shared a great deal about our lives and our beliefs. A female reporter for *Jewish Week* commented to me after talking with both of us, "You two work together so well. I really think only two women could have done this."

> *Paradoxically, by respectfully affirming and even celebrating our differences as people of faith, we moved closer together.*

Entitled "A Last Supper Celebration," the finished product was not designed to be an interfaith Seder although those are valid experiences. Instead, our liturgy borrowed from the form of a Seder but expressed Christian religious values and rituals while honoring the Seder's Jewish roots. We took the basic framework of the Seder—the story of the Exodus, the four cups, the unleavened bread—and reinterpreted them, in Jo's words, as a "vehicle for a more satisfying Christian spiritual linking with the Last Supper."

We required our confirmation students to attend and invited people of all faiths to participate as a learning experience. Over sixty people attended the meal, which was held exactly one week prior to Maundy Thursday. Despite the fears Jo and I expressed to each other, the response was overwhelmingly positive. Everyone was moved. At the end, no one

wanted to leave. Paradoxically, by respectfully affirming and even celebrating our differences as people of faith, we moved closer together.

Our purposes in creating the new liturgy were simple, but ripe with
interfaith implications. In an interview with a reporter from *Newsday,* Rabbi
Jo explained that we felt it is important for people of both faiths to see the
possibility of being inspired by a particular religious tradition and finding
a new spiritual path by using certain elements of that tradition rather than
just appropriating a whole tradition the way some churches do by saying,
"We're going to do a seder." Rabbi Jo had always felt uncomfortable with
churches taking a traditional Haggadah (the book used at a traditional
Jewish Seder) and struggling through the Hebrew, understanding it, but
not really understanding.

Recognizing Historic Pain

For my part as a Christian pastor, I hoped that my congregation members would have a richer understanding of the Jewish roots of Jesus' institution of the Last Supper. Even more, I hoped they would have learned
that as Christian and Jewish people of faith, we can join together and still
respect our differences. We need not co-opt one another's religious practices, but can learn from one another.

Also, as a Lutheran pastor, I remained aware of the treatment of the
Jewish people in Germany prior to and during World War II. Many of my
Jewish friends and acquaintances on Long Island are more aware than my
own church members of the direct and indirect anti-Semitic sentiments in
some of Martin Luther's writings. Of course, Luther was a product of his
times and anti-Semitism is not a Lutheran invention. Modern Lutherans
such as Dietrich Bonhoeffer were martyred for refusing to follow Hitler's
regime of hatred and violence against the Jews.

Not long ago, I was invited to another local synagogue as a guest
speaker. I spoke of Jesus' call for Christians to love their neighbors as they
love themselves. I expressed remorse for the ways some Christians abandoned their Jewish neighbors and friends during the Holocaust. Afterward,
a member of the synagogue came up to me with tears in his eyes saying,
"You will never know what it means to me to hear a Christian pastor say
what you did." This man was the son of a Holocaust survivor.

Lest we think anti-Semitism a thing of the past, in the two years I have
served as a pastor on Long Island, there have been numerous bias inci-
dents against Jews, including the defacing of temple property with a
swastika during Christian Holy Week. Nursery school children at Union
Reform Temple encountered the swastika on their way to school. As Rabbi
Jo and I planned this new liturgy, I was acutely aware that one of the steps

for peacemaking is to celebrate together. Respect flourishes when we clarify and affirm our differences as people of faith and yet still find a way to come together.

Reinterpreting Simple Rituals

Rabbi Jo explained the problems inherent in many Christian celebrations of the Pesach or Passover ritual. She said that it is unfortunate that many Christian clergy don't understand that what they are doing is very inaccurate. Their intentions are good but they may not realize how many Jews respond to this practice. She added that some Christians think they can just read from the Haggadah and it will be the same. People should know that much of the Haggadah as celebrated today was developed after Jesus lived, and that the Haggadah of Jesus' time was a much simpler ritual.

In contrast, our liturgy returned to the most basic elements of the Seder ritual and reinterpreted them. The four cups, for example, were dedicated to four people such as Dietrich Bonhoeffer and Rosa Parks who had helped liberate others. The four questions were reinterpreted to fit the purpose of the evening. In answer to, "How is this night different from all other nights?" a question asked by the youngest child at a traditional Seder, our liturgy responds: "On all other nights, we tell stories in the voices of the past, or speak of matters of concern in the present. On this night, we blend ancient and modern words and stories. We study the Jewish religious and historical components of the Last Supper and seek to incorporate these new insights into a deeper sense of Christian spiritual awareness."

Simple rituals such as hand-washing meant a great deal to those who attended. Jo explained the meaning of hand-washing at a traditional Seder. I explained that at Jesus' Last Supper, he washed the feet rather than the hands of his disciples. We invited each person to wash the hands of his or her neighbor at the table with a pitcher and bowl provided, while remembering Jesus' example of servanthood. Jesus said, "The greatest among you must become like the youngest, and the leader like one who serves" (Luke 22:26). Together, we sang "Jesu, Jesu," an African hymn about loving and serving one's neighbors. A member of my congregation later talked about seeing a woman tenderly and thoroughly wash the hands of the woman sitting next to her saying, "It brought tears to my eyes. It was so beautiful."

The mother of one of my confirmation students commented, "None of us had ever been to a Seder before, so we weren't sure what to expect, but Rabbi David and Pastor Wilson made it interesting and clear. The kids liked the ten plagues the best and they loved the desserts, even though they had a little trouble with the bitter herbs!" Another woman, a member of the cooking committee from Bethlehem Lutheran, observed, "Rabbi

David explained the Jewish traditions and Pastor Wilson discussed the relevance it had to our lives as Christians. The whole experience gave you a feeling of real closeness." A member of Union Reform Temple seconded, "Seeing the Seder from both sides was fascinating, especially the way they correlated the traditions. It was definitely done in a way where both Jews and Christians could learn from one another with neither side being offended."

There were a few bloopers along the way, however. My cooking committee was especially nervous about the food since they were unfamiliar with the recipes. Rabbi Jo laughed when she received a phone call several nights before the celebration, "It was the cooking committee wanting to know why the eggs they were roasting in the oven kept exploding." Roasted eggs are not a traditional Easter dish! We laughed together even as we learned, and the food was delicious. A special treat was the charoset, a mixture of apple, wine, and nuts, made as a reminder of the bricks and mortar the Israelites used to create in Egypt.

We ended our Last Supper Celebration with the Aaronic benediction given by me in English and by Rabbi Jo in Hebrew. Together, we said this statement of completion, "We came together tonight not knowing where this journey would lead us. We pray that God will be with each of us on our separate paths. Until we meet again, may the grace of God go with us." Psalm 133:1 helped form an excellent frame for this first Last Supper Celebration and for all the others that have followed: How very good and pleasant it is when kindred live together in unity!

CHAPTER TWENTY-THREE

Ordinary Kitchen: Campus Ministry

Alicia R. Anderson

In campus ministry or elsewhere one is called to minister to people individually and collectively, How do we engage in informal yet purposeful conversation? How do we help shape communities where each member is able to grow? Here is a specialized ministry in an ordinary place, a good place for sharing faith.

One of the advantages of running campus ministry out of an old farmhouse is that there is a kitchen. When I first arrived at the Campus Ministry Center on the edge of the University of Wisconsin-Whitewater campus, the kitchen itself was not spectacular, but it certainly was striking. There were ancient appliances, counters the brilliant color of grass after a summer rain, and wallpaper covered with fading yellow, orange, and green flowers. The white metal cabinets were yellowed with age, and the refrigerator had an unidentifiable and unpleasant odor. Sometime in the 1970s that room was considered beautiful, but the decor was dated and showing signs of wear.

This ugly kitchen, however, was the space where we prepared weekly dinners for students. We made chili and chicken and pasta and salad and potatoes and everything in between. Over the years I served there, the menus changed. We eventually settled on spaghetti, salad, and bread every week. It was a dependable, predictable meal with nothing to challenge the faint of heart; a dinner students could count on in the midst of an overwhelming week.

Community and Conversation

Before Christmas, this kitchen was the place we made cinnamon rolls and managed to spread flour absolutely everywhere. In the fall, it was the place where we served the "Thanksgiving Preview" dinner, and in the spring, it was the place where we prepared a Seder meal. Somehow, though, the food has relatively little to do with my memories of the kitchen at Whitewater. Though I spent many hours in the kitchen preparing meals or snacks, the food preparation seemed to be an almost mindless activity. Perhaps it seemed mindless because I saved my more adventurous

> **There we'd be, up to our elbows in dishwater.**

cooking experiences for my home kitchen, but I think it is more likely that the food was simply an excuse for the real reason we had gathered there. We came for community and conversation, support and feedback.

I cannot count the number of times students arrived early and offered to help, and while engaged in the chores of rinsing greens, cutting bread, or slicing cucumbers, they shared the struggles and troubles they had faced that week, or the complicated life-issues they were trying to discern. Other times, a student would offer to stay later to help wash and dry dishes and while we worked together, he or she would carve out a bit of quiet, one-on-one time with a campus minister. There we'd be, up to our elbows in dishwater and suds, talking about broken relationships with roommates and friends, a dad who had lost his job, or a new major and a new course in life. We would talk about questions of spiritual and denominational identity or about God's will for vocation. Of course, there was plenty of joking, laughter, and lighthearted routine, signs of the connections and the love that lived in the kitchen and the Campus Ministry Center.

As we stood there, side by side, stirring pasta, we gave a unique kind of support. No eye contact was required, but it certainly was available if a student wanted a reassuring look. Talking while working together can be so much less threatening than making an appointment to sit down for a closed-door session. Preparing a meal, or cleaning up can be a casual, comfortable time where it may not even seem like someone is seeking pastoral care.

Students and Staff

Even when meals weren't involved, the kitchen was a place where people found community and support. It served as the gathering place for a woman's discussion group during several semesters. We actually met in the back room, but since we talked over tea, we started our time together in the kitchen, waiting for the water in the kettle to boil. Women scattered around the room, choosing tea bags, mixing cocoa. Someone usually sat on the counter, someone often rooted through the cabinet hoping for a better tea flavor, and someone was always trying to find a burner that would light. Here in the kitchen, women would begin to share their thoughts and concerns about the church and women's roles within it, higher education and its effects on women, faith journeys, the complexity of sexuality, the role of relationships, concepts of God, the ways women mentors guide and lead, and much more. It always seemed appropriate to me that these conversations began in the kitchen. For generations, women have had these very conversations in kitchens around the world.

I shared much with my colleague, Jim, in this kitchen. We laughed and cried there many times over the years. One night, I sat on the counter and wept while I poured my heart out to him, finding counsel, support, and guidance. Other times, as we shared coffee or lunch we also shared our lives, our concerns for the students, ideas about our ministry, or struggles with our denominations. We built community and established the kind of connections that last a lifetime.

At one point, Jim and I decided to paint the kitchen while we were doing some other work in the building. On Friday afternoon, I left for an hour while our student worker and Jim began removing the wallpaper. When I returned, I found they'd decided it would be easier to simply remove the wallboard. Weeks later, we had gutted the kitchen. It was down to ceiling joists and studs. Jim and I encountered different challenges to staff ministry as we hung the drywall and waited for the new appliances to be installed.

Today the kitchen is much different in appearance. The floor is new, the counters are bright, and the appliances are modern and don't smell. Of course, it is still not the perfect kitchen. The cabinets are unstained, the floor gets dirty too quickly, and there isn't nearly enough storage space. But this kitchen is still the place where endless pots of pasta and sauce are prepared and served. Laughter and conversation and big life-questions are shared over meals and dishes.

New Places and Possibilities

Although I continue to serve in campus ministry, I am now serving on a campus in central Pennsylvania. We do some of our work here out of an old house. We gather for meals and meetings, but the kitchen doesn't seem to serve the same role. It isn't a passageway into the rest of the house. It doesn't have the warmth or charm of the kitchen I left, and it hasn't become a place for personal, yet public, conversation. It still is a place where community is built, but it is not a place for informal pastoral care. We have fewer opportunities for that kind of informal conversation, and I continue to look for ways to be available to students "in the midst of things."

I've begun to see that while our kitchen here in Pennsylvania doesn't work for informal pastoral care, other places can. This fall, in a Habitat for Humanity house under construction, I taught a student how to put joint compound into the seams between the drywall and to make a perfect corner. As we stood on stools in opposite corners of the room, we talked about his studies, his career, the communities of faith that have touched his life, his hopes for the future, and laughed at the fact that we both were covered in joint compound. Weeks later, I found myself with students talking about men's and women's roles on a Habitat workday where some were irritated by the site coordinator's discrimination between genders as he gave out jobs.

Students and I have talked about community needs and social inequity while sorting clothes at the nearby clothes closet, and about families, poverty, and favorite foods while handing out food at the food bank. While students taught me to play gin and hearts late at night at a retreat or conference, they've talked with me about struggles in life, concepts of God, or the way they've been hurt by their families. After a speaker's address at a conference, students shared an emotional conversation on the floor about how challenging they were finding these ideas and perspectives, while the conference center staff rearranged the room around us.

Of course I also have had meaningful conversations with students who have arranged a time to meet with me in my office. We've talked about the whole spectrum of life issues there with the door closed. But there is a special character to the meaningful conversations that have taken place in less expected places. Those are conversations that sprang out of the moment, conversations that were possible because of trust and a shared connection around things we were doing. Those are conversations that grew out of the safety of having something else to do while we talked.

In campus ministry we often share the joke, "If you feed them, they will come." The conversations that take place in the kitchen and those other ordinary spaces may reflect the core of ministry. In the midst of carrying out a task, we engage in so much more. Meals are prepared, buildings are built, food and clothes are sorted while community is built, hearts are healed, spirits are soothed, pains are expressed, comfort is given, and relationships are built.

The surroundings may differ, but still we are doing so much more than just making dinner.

CHAPTER TWENTY-FOUR

Ordinary Images: The Ministry of Oversight

Andrea DeGroot-Nesdahl

How can we lead in ways so that people do not become unnecessarily dependent upon us? What is the ministry of leadership and vision? Three images provide insights for our personal lives and our public ministry of carrying out responsibilities with balance and joy. In reimagining her bishop's role, Andrea helps the church reshape leadership itself.

A Spider Beside My Mirror

I was standing at my bedroom mirror at the end of a long day. Tired. Preparing to go to bed. Savoring the quiet, the solitude. No one asking me to make conversation. Out of the corner of my eye, I saw a spider on the wall beside the mirror. I stood there a full thirty seconds, considering my options.

First option: I could run, screaming, out of the room as I did when I was a child, searching then for my father to be my hero and rescue me. "Take away the scary thing, Daddy! Make it better!" I am now forty-eight years old, an adult woman, a mother, a pastor, and a bishop. Why do I still, always, think first of running away, screaming? This is no longer an option. It's not that my husband wouldn't accommodate me; rather, it's that I no longer have much room for the child inside.

177

Second option vis-à-vis the spider: I remember when my children were younger and saw an insect in the house. They just left the room, or sometimes the entire part of the house where the insect was. "We can't go into the bedroom, Mommy. There's a bug in there." Why do such small problems or insects or spiders have such power? The option of leaving my bedroom and never returning because there was a spider on the wall didn't seem feasible. It was bedtime; I was tired. This is my sanctuary; I don't want to give it up.

Third option: Just go to bed and forget about it. Would it be possible to just coexist with the spider? My bedroom seemed large enough for the both of us, on the surface, anyway. But could I really rest knowing this enemy was afoot (afeet?)? I felt some obligation to protect the rest of the house. What if the spider didn't bother me, but went into other rooms . . . the children's for example? Then I would be the parent to whom they would come screaming. I realized as a homeowner and a parent that I was responsible for the whole house, not just for my own room. I had to handle this problem before it spread.

I killed the spider.

Reflection

What kind of allegory on leadership in the church was this experience? If the bedroom was a congregation, and I the pastor of it, what would my spider options say about leadership? Option one: Do I see a small thing that I identify as a problem, and give it more power than it merits? Do I react to problems by screaming and running for help, when I am capable of problem-solving myself? Perhaps, as a child, I received much more from my dad than just spider termination. I also received his personal attention. He came to my room; we probably talked for awhile as he reassured me and made me feel safe again. It seems perfectly normal for a child to need those things from a parent; however, it doesn't seem healthy when a pastor as an adult wants some outside authority to meet those kinds of childhood security and love needs. Neither is it healthy when congregations want that kind of relationship from their pastor, with the pastor serving as a rescuer or hero.

Option two: Sometimes in conflict situations people just leave the room, figuratively speaking. They just leave the church, close the door, and say they can't go back there because there is a problem inside. Pastors do the same. A leader has a difficult role staying in the room with the problem. This reminds me of hospital calls early in my pastoral ministry. When I was told that a person was near death and I went to see that individual, I could sense a physical pull toward the door of the room. I was so afraid of being there when death came, I literally felt drawn to leave. I remember the discipline it took to stay. I needed to remind myself to breathe normally as the patient began to breathe erratically and, finally, to die. Prayer and experience taught me how powerful those ministry moments are. How important it is to stay through the fear. How much peace there can be in accompanying someone to that threshold of new life. I know more now about what I would miss by leaving the room. So it is with problem-solving: to stay and deal with the problem holds more potential for being peace-filled than shutting doors and never reentering.

Option three: Coexisting with the problem. On the plus side, this builds tolerance, which seems to be in short supply in our culture. On the negative side, this stalwart approach can foster individualism: "If you don't bother me, I won't bother you." This response is antithetical to the concept of the church as a community. Our reluctance to identify a problem as such and to cope with it often allows it to multiply and spread. Rather than dealing with a negative situation in a life-giving way, congregations that perceive that a member is a problem often simply hope that by ignoring or merely tolerating that person they will buy themselves peace. Or they hope that the person causing the problem may simply leave, go to another room, so to speak, and therefore not be this congregation's problem anymore. It is rare for congregations to see themselves in relationship to the whole church, having responsibility and accountability to others. Congregations are more inclined to see themselves as islands or kingdoms separate from others.

In rural ministry we work hard at redefining that autonomous and independent sense of congregation. We try to teach and model a common witness and common faith stance that fosters clustering and realigning and cooperation. I am often amazed by the propensity of members, pastors, and congregations as a whole to deny reality. This would be akin to my saying, "I'm going to sleep; there is not a spider in my room."

My encouragement to leaders, lay and clergy alike, is to stay in the room with the problems long enough to see what the options for resolution and future mission are, then make informed decisions and move on. Spiders on the wall, like any problem in life, are not the end of the world. God will always lead us through any difficulty.

Canning Pears in My Kitchen

One day while canning pears, I peeled the fruit, gradually filling the quart jars that ultimately would go into the open-kettle canner on top of the stove to boil for at least twenty minutes. I noted happily that I was using all four burners at one time. But there was nothing in the oven. Since

179

I was in the kitchen, and had a little time between filling jars and removing processed jars from boiling water, I made some banana bread for the oven. I regretted that I had run the dishwasher the night before, and therefore did not yet have enough dishes to run another load.

During another brief pause in the canning process, just before the banana bread was done, I needed to run downstairs for something. Out of habit, I glanced into the laundry room on my way by. Hmmm . . . dirty clothes. I realized that I could throw in a load of clothes on

> *I see congregations programming themselves at an increasingly faster pace.*

my way back up. I mentally tallied that in several hours I could have twenty-one quarts of canned pears, fresh banana bread, and several loads of clean clothes, which, if you counted the clean dishes from last night in the dishwasher, added up to a respectable total of completed projects in one day.

I was warming up to the idea on my way back up when I caught sight of myself in the bathroom mirror. It was not a Martha Stewart moment. I looked driven, tense, half-angry (which resembles half-mad). The whole point of canning was to enjoy the process. I look forward to it all year. I plan my schedule around the fruit being in season and available. I prepare ahead of time: jars, lids, rings, sugar, prize recipe from Mom. Canning is a family tradition I am proud to carry on, although I was over forty, and serving as an assistant to a bishop, when I first decided to learn. I visited my parents' home and watched my mother; she had canned for so long and so well that she had no written recipe. So Dad sat at the kitchen counter as scribe for the process. His commentary, complete with, "Serve with warm bread on a cold, snowy night," has become precious to me, especially since he died the next year. The process and the relationship is so much more important than the product. So how do I become so caught up in needing to do more and more? Why do I need end-of-the-day totals?

Pause

I see congregations, especially in fast-growing areas, programming themselves at an increasingly faster pace. Lay leaders are caught up in planning and scheduling more and more for every conceivable group and constituency. Pastors compete with themselves to provide more ministries, more services in more formats, more statistics about more trends, needs, and issues. What does it mean to be the church in this fast-paced age? How do we nurture ministers to pace themselves and their congregations for the long haul?

Ministers encourage growth in discipleship. We try to help people remember, as well as to mind the disciplines of Christian life: worship, prayer, offering, service, learning. How are those being modeled and balanced in our overall church program? How do we nurture lay leaders in their volunteer roles in the church so that they reflect back on this experience as a time of growth in their faith, not just another pressure on their schedules?

Jesus so often pulled away from the crowds in order to become renewed. He rested in order to interact with them again. We need to model ourselves after his example. We can live with an ebb and flow rather than a steady pounding. Next canning season, I'm going to focus on "pearing" down my schedule.

Soaring Above the Earth

My assistant to the bishop, Jeff, and I encountered the first blizzard of the season on the way home from a "Hope for the Prairie" event in Aberdeen. "Hope," at the moment, meant much more mundane things like being able to see the road, not sliding on the ice, and not encountering another vehicle that was out of control because of the weather. Hope revolved around that which was literally right in front of us: around the "local conditions." Miles would pass of less-than-perfect winter driving conditions and then the local conditions would change, the road would clear, and visibility would improve. Hope soared: We would get all the way home tonight!

And we did get home, just in time to be thoroughly snowed in the next two days. Then there were big drifts of heavy, wet snow to be cleared, with icy roads underneath, and blustery winds and chilling cold! I was so grateful not to be on the road somewhere. And then I remembered that on the road I often drive through "local conditions." And here at home I also have to live with them. My hope is always that the "conditions" will leave me or my locale.

It reminded me of labor pains. The theory is that the birthing mother will completely relax and wait calmly for the next pain to begin, to peak, and to subside. She will be able to breathe through the pain in such a way that she is detached from its real power and stays focused on the goal: the baby's coming. Many mothers remember that about halfway through that birthing process we just wanted to get up and go home. No more relaxing and calm waiting and disciplined focus through the increasingly more painful labor. We want to drive quickly through the "local conditions" rather than breathe through them until they pass.

All of that crossed my mind at the end of that blizzard week when I flew in a small plane to a regional meeting near Alexandria, Minnesota. We left

181

the snow and ice, the rough roads and potholes, the varying degrees of slush and slick and soared above the earth. We were just high enough to see the big picture, to regain perspective. It was a stunning day to fly: bright winter sunshine, clean, snow-covered landscape and, as always, the wonderful orderliness of the land itself. We viewed neatly squared fields; straight, paved highways and artful cloverleafs. Small clustered homes and businesses with toylike trains and tracks and water towers and elevators huddled together and glistened in the morning sun. Our churches are not only beautiful on the ground, they are truly magnificent from the air. They seem to command respect and focus by their spires, their stature, and their cemeteries.

Perspective

I thought about perspective from days in parish ministry when I would stand in front of a congregation on a Sunday morning. I thought of how I needed to see the people as a group, especially if it had been a week when the needs or crises of one or two families had just plain overwhelmed my days and my senses. On Sunday, they seemed whole, not just parts that make up the whole. There was a fullness about the picture that I both felt and understood when I saw the congregation together on a Sunday morning.

I had that sense of perspective flying in the small plane. I enjoyed the ride; I was out of the post-blizzard conditions. Seeing several communities at the same time, knowing there were churches in them, and between them, was a little like standing in front of the congregation. It was more like seeing the whole rather than the individual parts of local conditions. I was, for a little while, seeing something God sees all the time. That perspective helps me understand why God would become a human baby and dwell among us, full of grace and truth. God wants to land, and will live among us—rough roads, pain, complexity, and all.

CHAPTER TWENTY-FIVE

Ordinary Prayer: The Ministry of Outreach

Ann E. Helmke

The church is called to come outside locked doors, to open our arms so we can pray with and for the world. In a society trapped in its own fascination with violence, how do we build community? Where do we begin when people are too afraid to care? Outside

Violence may be titillating, but prayer is transformative. That's what I discovered one hot August in San Antonio.

Early that month the ten o'clock newscasts and the local newspaper were filled with images of one of the most violent acts that had ever occurred in that city. A father, his teenage daughter, and three other teenage friends had all been brutally murdered in a home, execution style. The media images that flashed before us were body bags, a home in one of the poorest sections in the city, and the tear-stained faces of the victims' families. The images were horrifying and the loss to our community was devastating. Most disconcerting, though, was the collective excitement throughout the city that seemed to circle this horrific event. It was uncanny and almost unexplainable.

As I would go about my work during that week, I continually met people who were talking about the situation, or rather the media event. Yet it wasn't talk about what we could do or the great loss, it was speculation about the murders and talk about the gruesome details. People were drawn to and excited by such violence.

Haunting Images

Even more disconcerting was the lack of concern, of healing, or of wholeness. As I would roam around the city and hear people talking about the event, I would rarely hear anyone mention what people of faith were doing about this tragedy. It was a huge absence of concern in the abyss of much hurt.

The images haunted me. I couldn't get them out of my head. I kept thinking, "There's got to be something we can do. Such violence is pulling us apart as a community and there is nothing that is pulling us together. Where's the faith community?" I would ponder and pray each day about what we could do. Yet nothing came to mind. By the end of the day, I would have almost convinced myself that there was nothing that I could do as one person in the middle of the tenth largest city in the country. It was a struggle to go to sleep with those images. Just as surely as I had convinced myself the night before that there was nothing that I could do, I would wake up each morning convicted that something must be done!

Out of such searching prayer the answer came: more prayer! An earlier memory was sparked. I remembered a dear friend telling me about prayer vigils being held at sites of violence in another city where he had visited. He had shared with me the simplicity of the vigils, the historic precedence, and the potential impact that prayer vigils might have within our own community. However, as luck would have it, my knowledgeable friend was on vacation and I had no idea how to pull together a prayer vigil! More prayer was needed.

The idea came to call twelve (a good biblical number) leaders across the city. They needed to be folks who could quickly understand the need *and* the concept. The calls were not meant to be "sales" calls, but invitations into ordinary prayer and an extraordinary way to be community. Each of the twelve was invited and given power to invite others—from every corner of the city, every economic level, every faith tradition, every age bracket, and every culture. Like the women at the foot of the cross or at the tomb, I could feel the potential for healing and ministry throughout my entire body! "God, *teach* us to pray" became my new litany.

The vigil was set for Sunday evening at sundown. We encouraged people to bring candles, bring friends, and bring family to the place where the five had died. Early in the invitation process, I decided that the quantity of the pray-ers was not important; that coming together to pray was important. Knowing as I do the sheer power of Spirit and prayer, I should not have been surprised at the numbers of people who came to pray, but I was awestruck. As I drove up to the site that evening, the litany filled my entire body, "God, teach us to *pray.*"

Without any notification, all of the major media were there. I became concerned that it was about to become a media event instead of a prayer event. "They" were going to ruin the full potential of the gathering. However, the fact that "they" were there might indicate a desire to report and show other images besides blood-stained floors, body bags, and victims screaming for justice to be served. After more prayer, I tried to center on the fact that God works through all things, and decided to greet media with arms wide open. It was an attempt to diffuse any media distraction from the real purpose for gathering: prayer.

Unlocked Doors

As the crowd gathered and while I talked with the media, I began to realize that neighbors of this violated home were peering out through their doors and windows. The media seemed sincerely curious—as curious as the peering eyes of the neighbors. Once the media received up-front information, my attention turned toward those gathering and the window watchers. The words, "go and tell" came to mind. I encountered family members of one of the teen victims. Initially they had planned not to attend this gathering or ever return to this house. Some power within encouraged them to do otherwise. As I listened to their story and their pain, my heart swelled and I knew that Christ was in our midst. Their faith and fortitude empowered me to go door to door down the street. There must be pain and fear there as well.

It was true. Many of the neighbors had not been out of their homes except to go to work and to buy groceries since the tragedy. My heart kept repeating the litany, "teach us to *pray*." One by one, two by two, family by family, babies and elders, every skin tone, men, women, Christians, Jews, Muslims, and others—they came. One newspaper reporter counted over 120 people. That's tenfold the original guest list! God is so good. It was a hot August night in Texas but it was nothing compared to the warmth of the hearts of the people who gathered in a circle on that front lawn. The site was cross and tomb all rolled up in one. During the welcome, I encouraged people to form a circle, to "get close" and surround the family members with bodily support.

Before my gentle reminder that we were many faith traditions gathered in common unity with common purpose, I noticed that we were actually encircling four large television cameras! I leaned over to a friend and said, "The last thing I want to do is pray over TV cameras and the media." My friend lovingly responded, "I thought you said anyone could come and pray. Maybe they need prayer, too." This was a moment of personal transformation. I had perceived the media as intrusive instead of as fellow community members also in need of healing and prayer. I had labeled them

"them," "those people," and "media" instead of seeing fellow creations of God in all of their humanity.

Since that moment of simultaneous conviction and conversion, I welcome people who work within the mass media as fellow travelers on a life journey—a journey where we share struggles and sorrows and a search for hope and healing. My heart was disarmed and I felt mutual prayer and transformation. Once again, the litany came, "Teach *us* to pray." Finally, candles were lit and collectively we began to pray—randomly by human standards; inspired by holy standards. There were prayers for the victims and those who had performed the violence—that both might find peace, reconciliation, and a sense of God's restorative justice. There were prayers for the neighborhood and the very dirt we stood on—that God's Spirit might bless this place with healing love. There were prayers for the entire city, for churches and synagogues, for people of faith—that they stand strong and not be afraid to show their faith to the world. There were prayers that the cycle of violence be replaced with circles of peace. Family members read poems. Tears were shed by all. Candles flickered, blew out, and were re-lit from others' candles. Prayers rose like incense. Hearts opened and healing began. Prayer, blessed prayer, began the transformation.

Each time there was a lull I called forth for "any more prayers." More prayers followed until a most amazing thing happened. Without anyone's prompting, some-

> **The place that had been violated became holy ground.**

one began singing "Amazing Grace." By the third note all were singing. A procession began to form and encircle the home. By now it was dark and the candles flickered in the night. People walked arm in arm, singing, praying silently. Some were laying their hands upon the weathered wood siding. Some were pushing their lit candles into the dirt near the foundation of the home. It took my breath away!

The place that had been so violated just one week before became holy ground. The almost sacramental scene helped me to realize that in our death-denying culture we sterilize and detach ourselves as much as possible from the dying process. We need to see, touch, and feel death in order to really live!

Following the vigil that lasted almost two hours, family members locked arms in the front yard. They sang boldly in harmony with taped music flowing out of one of their cars. When the tape ran out, someone ran back to the car and rewound the tape so they could sing again. They sang. They held each other. They cried. They laughed. Others joined in.

Neighbors congregated on the sidewalk. All admitted it was the best they had felt in a week. Since they had been too afraid to come out of their homes, they had not realized that others were also suffering. They made plans among themselves to continue their conversation and concerns by meeting regularly in one another's homes. Other ideas, like house blessings, were explored. The eyes that earlier that evening were hesitantly peeking out of windows were now filled with sparkle and hope for the future. They, and we, were different people than when we first arrived. Even the leadoff stories on the nightly news were filled with prayer and hope. These were far different images from those we had been watching the entire week prior. Truly a transformation!

More Prayer Vigils

Many more prayer vigils have occurred since that hot August night. It's not unusual for churches or family members or friends of those who have suffered some form of violence to arrange a vigil. Prayer vigils at sites of violence are a contagious model of ministry in the community. It's such a simple, ordinary ministry with the outcome being extraordinary grace!

Though I'm risking the label of heretic, it all makes me ponder and wonder if, as Christians, we have too quickly glossed over some very critical words in Luke 11. For almost two millennia we have faithfully and collectively recited the words of the Lord's Prayer. Maybe, just maybe, the critical life-transforming words in the passage are, "Teach us to pray." The original Twelve obviously witnessed something in Jesus' life that they desired for their own lives—the power of prayer to transform! Maybe that's what the Gospel writer wanted future readers and followers to hear: don't be afraid to pray; it's essential to the faith journey; Jesus was a great prayer model; and prayer is a definite action that can be learned! It may be two thousand years later, but the message still holds true. Violence may be titillating, but prayer is transformative.

CONTRIBUTORS

PART ONE

1. Rebecca A. Ellenson serves as one of four pastors on a large staff at First Lutheran Church in Duluth, Minnesota. Prior to this call, she served for four years as a solo pastor in an open-country parish in southern Minnesota. Rebecca is married and has two children. She volunteers as a ski instructor at a local resort and practices karate regularly. She highly recommends karate as an excellent stress reliever, commenting, "Where else can a grown woman go twice a week to punch and kick and yell for an hour and a half?"

2. Sandra Moen Kennedy, a former schoolteacher and parish worker, is now a pastor serving the shared ministry of Hope Lutheran Church in Homer City, Pennsylvania, and New Life Lutheran Church, near Marion Center, Pennsylvania. These congregations are a reorganized parish (formerly five churches) twenty miles apart in Indiana County, which is marked with coal mines, Christmas tree farming, and power plants. Sandra continues her ministry of grief work as volunteer Spiritual Counselor with Family Hospice of Indiana County. She also serves the patients of Torrance State Hospital as chaplain, which she considers a special blessing in her life. A source of strength, encouragement, and humor are her children Rachel (twenty-one), Jessica (nineteen), and Patrick (eighteen).

3. Holly W. Whitcomb has been a clergywoman in the United Church of Christ since her graduation from Yale Divinity School in 1978. She also completed a two-year training program for spiritual directors. A widely traveled retreat leader, Holly is the founder of Kettlewood Retreats, a ministry of spiritual formation near Milwaukee. She has published more than fifty resources and is the author of a book, *Feasting with God*. She lives in a suburb of Milwaukee with her husband and their teenage children. Holly has begun practicing Sabbath, frequently incorporating her blissful hobby of jewelry making. She loves the flash and fire of beads and gemstones so much that it helps her lose track of time.

4. Mary Jo Maass currently serves as pastor in rural/small town ministry with the people of God at Immanuel Lutheran Church in Mediapolis, Iowa. In 1992–93 she was an exchange student at the Lutheran Theological College in Makumira, Tanzania. Recently, as a representative of the Southeastern Iowa Synod, she participated in a companion synod consultation in Arusha, Tanzania, with representatives of other Evangelical Lutheran Church in America synods and Evangelical Lutheran Church in Tanzania dioceses. The goal was to envision and plan how people can walk together *bega kwa bega* (shoulder to shoulder) into the twenty-first century. Mary Jo is the mother of three grown children and "bibi" to two grandchildren.

5. Kris Ann Zierke for six years has been pastor of a rural Lutheran two-point parish (Zion and Trinity) in Adams County, Wisconsin, her first call since ordination. Before seminary, she served for four years as a deaconess in Iowa. In addition to current pastoral responsibilities, Kris directs the choir for one of the churches (and enjoys learning new music for worship). Because she strongly believes she is called to serve the community as well as the congregation, Kris is involved in numerous community services, including the Adams County W-2 Steering Committee (welfare reform), Community Children's Concern Committee, and the Hospital Bio-ethics Committee.

6. Kathryn K. J. Gerking is a Pastoral Assistant to the Bishop and Mission Director in the Southeastern Iowa Synod of the Evangelical Lutheran Church in America. Previously she served as pastor of a small-town church for seven years. Her husband, Andy, assumed full-time household responsibilities when Kathy took her present call. He recently began a part-time job, which has led them to another evaluation of shared ministry, shared life, shared parenting (of Ann [ten] and Aaron [five]), and balance.

Barbara J. Bullock-Tiffany was diagnosed with and died from cancer during the time this book was in preparation. Barbara served as pastor of Immanuel Lutheran Church in Camanche, Iowa, for four years. Barbara, wife to the Rev. Douglas Bullock-Tiffany, and mother to Eric, received her Master of Divinity degree from Wartburg Theological Seminary in Dubuque, Iowa, and her doctorate in music from the University of Iowa. She played second clarinet in the Quad City Symphony Orchestra for many years, was an accomplished organist, and wrote several musical compositions.

PART TWO

7. Barbara J. Knutson is pastor of Oakland Lutheran Church in Albert Lea, Minnesota, and Moscow Lutheran Church in Austin, Minnesota. Prior to ordination, she served for thirty-one years as an associate in ministry in three parishes in North Dakota, Wisconsin, and Montana, on the national staff of the American Lutheran Church, and as assistant to the bishop of the Southwestern Minnesota District (ALC) and Synod (ELCA). Last year she led Easter vigil for the first time at Moscow. This year a nearby large congregation called to say, "We can't hold an Easter vigil because we can't build a fire in the city and we don't have a cemetery for the 'Pascal candle parade.' Could we invite ourselves to Moscow?" Barbara says that the subsequent joint-planning was wonderful.

8. Mary A. Rowland is part of the mutual ministry team at Reformation Church (ELCA) in the heart of Milwaukee. Previous ministry included youth ministry for seven years in Iowa, Christian education in the Lutheran Church in Guyana, and pastoral ministry at a suburban partner church to Reformation. A key to ordinary ministry becoming extraordinary, in her experience, is the trusting and prayerful relationships of Reformation's specific team and the larger coalition in Milwaukee. She feels it is a joy to work for God with colleagues so open to new ideas that they say, "I don't quite get it, Mary, but if you say so. . . ."

9. Carol J. Rask is a homemaker who has lived in Maquoketa, Iowa, since 1965 with her husband, Clifford, who is now semi-retired from his family medical practice. Carol has long been active in a variety of church and community activities. She received her master of arts degree from seminary in 1981. As a continuing advocate for women, she recently asked for, and received, time on a local talk show to discuss the importance of using inclusive language in everyday life. "I was distressed over the demeaning of women by newscasters and some guests on our local radio talk shows." In addition to her daughter, Karen, Carol has a grown son, Tim.

Karen Rask Behling serves as pastor of Concordia Lutheran Church of Pickerel Lake (near Albert Lea), Minnesota. She previously served as associate pastor of St. John Evangelical Lutheran Church in Charles City, Iowa, and as pastor of Fordville Lutheran Parish, a three-point parish in North Dakota. She and husband David are parents to Marta (ten), Stuart (five), and Emma (three), who are learning well the stories they hear when they sometimes join Mama for nursing home and shut-in visits.

10. April Ulring Larson has been serving as Bishop of the LaCrosse (Wisconsin) Area Synod (ELCA), since 1992. She was the first woman to be elected as bishop in the Evangelical Lutheran Church in America. She previously served as Assistant to the Bishop, Southeastern Minnesota Synod, following eleven years as parish pastor. Her husband, the Rev. Judd Larson, recently took a new full-time call to Bethel Lutheran Church in La Crosse. April recently completed a three-month sabbatical, and was grateful during that time to be able to attend the same church every Sunday with Judd and her youngest child, Ben (fifteen), to direct choral music again, to receive seven to eight hours of sleep a night, and to eat regular meals. April and Judd's twin daughters, Katie and Amy, are twenty-one and loving college.

11. Virginia Anderson-Larson is the lead pastor at Zion Lutheran Church in Davenport, Iowa. Ginger also has served as Associate Pastor at Zion, and as a co-pastor with her husband, Keith, in a two-point, open country/small town parish. Prior to seminary she was a physical education teacher and also taught in Tolagnara, Madagascar. She recently completed a three-month sabbatical, with a study focus on "Faith Formation in Families," which included a ten-day pilgrimage of reverse mission to Haiti. Ginger and Keith are parents of three sons: Benjamin (twenty-two), Zachary (twenty), and Samuel (sixteen).

12. Norma Cook Everist is Professor of Church and Ministry at Wartburg Theological Seminary in Dubuque, Iowa, where she has taught for twenty-one years. She is an author and lecturer, and previously taught for three years at Yale Divinity School. She has served parishes in St. Louis, Detroit, New Haven, and Hamden, Connecticut. Norma is a pastor and also continues to be a member of the Lutheran Deaconess Community. She and her husband, Burton, are parents of three adult sons: Mark, Joel, and Kirk. She has been privileged to be both teacher and friend to many of these women authors, most recently visiting Karen Weissenbuehler in Denver, where she indeed found much hope!

PART THREE

13. Marj Leegard still lives on the land where she and Jerome, her husband of fifty-seven years, have farmed since 1944. Marj, who describes herself as "semi-retired," travels frequently to speaking engagements around the country. She has been a columnist for *Lutheran Woman Today* since 1994. She has written a 125th anniversary history of her congregation, a stewardship booklet, *Thankful Stewards,* and a book of her stories, *Give Us This Day*. This day (when this description was written) Marj took pussy willows to a nursing home and corresponded with a Texas legislator who requested a copy of a speech she delived at a "Seeds of Hope on the Prairie" conference.

14. Linda L. Ridgeway lives in Detroit and has been a member of and volunteer youth director at Springfield Baptist Church for forty-six years. The children of Linda and Booker T. range in age from twenty to forty-one. Although Linda is retired from employment in an automotive firm, she continues to reach out to neighborhood youth with the gospel. Last October Linda was invited once again to direct the children's choir at her church. They rehearse every Saturday and sing every second Sunday. She says of all the youth among whom she has ministered, "You have to be with them at all stages of the journey."

15. Rhonda R. Hanisch is Associate Pastor of Ascension Lutheran Church in Brookings, South Dakota, after having served Badger Lutheran Church in Badger, South Dakota, for six years. Before becoming a pastor she earned a master's degree in English from the University of South Dakota. Rhonda has served as conference dean for forty-one area congregations. She is currently part of the planning team for the next national youth gathering for her church body. Rhonda enjoys fishing and has been named "The Carp Queen of Lake Kampeska" by her fellow anglers for catching a carp weighing twenty-nine pounds, ten ounces.

16. Sandy Berg-Holte serves both as Pastor of CornerStone Ministries and Case Coordinator at CornerStone Supportive Transitional Housing Program near Wahkon, Minnesota. Birthing a new specialized ministry in a non-traditional mission field has been and continues to be a faith walk for Sandy. Sharing a vision, telling the story, building support, and working for social change and justice are all part of the challenges. Sandy now faces another new challenge: Within the next two years the housing program will have to rebuild, since the present facilities have been sold. Sandy and her husband, Jim, have three children: Brian (fourteen), Emily, (eleven), and Janelle (eight). They live near Aitkin, Minnesota.

17. Maryann Cox Morgenstern is Co-pastor, with her spouse, Mark, of Pella Lutheran Church in Sidney, Montana. She celebrates ministry in rural Montana with the members of her family still at home: Crystal (sixteen), Emilie (fifteen), and Tasha, the family cat. Maryann and Mark have regular "laundry visits" from their children in college: Curt (nineteen) and Aaron (eighteen). Daughter Gretchen (twenty-three) lives up the road. Maryann daily takes in the Big Sky expanse with her horses Abe, Socks, and Goldie. This past year Maryann had the opportunity to donate a kidney to a friend in the congregation. "Life is full of celebrations and growing edges that keep us proclaiming and living the good news of our Triune God!"

18. Sr. Mary Owen Haggerty, O.P. is the Parish Health Minister for two small churches in East Dubuque, Illinois: Grace Lutheran and Wesley United Methodist. She served previously as nursing supervisor and health consultant throughout the United States for the Dominican Sisters of Sinsinawa, Wisconsin. She has been a member of that community for forty-eight years and a registered nurse for fifty. For six years she spent two weeks a year working with Medical Ministry International in rural Jamaica. Recently she spent a month in Alaska caring for two Sisters recovering from surgery, and marveling at the Alaskan winter beauty.

19. Kathryn Bielfeldt is Pastor of St. John Lutheran Church in Campbell Hill, Illinois, and works with another pastor in a shared ministry with two other congregations. In late spring last year her faithful companion, Zephaniah, died. Kathryn's adjustment to living without her guide dog has been difficult. She recently was a delegate at both the national convention of the women of her church body and the churchwide assembly. Together with a group of local pastors she plans to participate in a bike-a-thon for youth social services; she is looking for someone with whom to ride tandem. "I'll steer, they can pedal," she quips.

191

PART FOUR

20. Karen Weissenbuehler is Pastor of Good Shepherd Lutheran Church in Denver, Colorado. Previously she was an associate pastor in Longmont, Colorado. She earned a master's degree in music/organ performance from the University of Denver in 1975. Working as a music teacher at an area high school and serving in downtown shelters and agencies prepared her to be pastor of a redeveloping congregation. The recent birth of granddaughter Rebekah reminds Karen, "We all stand on the shoulders of those who precede us; our ministry is just a small part of a congregation's life." Karen intends to remain as Pastor at Good Shepherd for a few years while the congregation moves toward greater stability.

21. Christine E. Iverson, a pastor under full-time call to Lutheran Disaster Response through Lutheran Social Service of Kansas-Oklahoma, is responsible for direct disaster response, worship resources, consultation, care for the caregiver, and development of children's materials. Together with her husband, the Rev. Valerian Ahles, she served four congregations in west-central Kansas and has also served five interim pastorates. She has facilitated rural social science education courses through Texas A&M University. She is concerned about rural America, the farm crisis, and the rise of hate groups and militia activity. Christine and Valerian have two grown sons in college and one daughter at home.

22. Kimberly A. Wilson is Pastor of Bethlehem Lutheran Church in Baldwin, New York, on Long Island. Bethlehem is the first church she has served as pastor. Prior to attending seminary, Kim worked as Associate Director of Development at Habitat for Humanity International in Americus, Georgia. She currently serves as the president of her local Clergy Interfaith Fellowship Group in Baldwin. She recently completed a continuing education course on creative writing. In addition to writing sermons, she enjoys writing short stories and poems.

23. Alicia R. Anderson is Lutheran Campus Minister at Penn State University in central Pennsylvania. Previously she served in campus ministry at the University of Wisconsin-Whitewater and the University of Nebraska-Lincoln. Alicia is currently an Associate in Ministry in the Evangelical Lutheran Church in America and is a candidate for diaconal ministry. In her life and ministry she continues to look for kitchens and other ordinary places where community is just waiting to be built. Alicia lives with her daughter, Jessa (seven), outside State College, Pennsylvania.

24. Andrea DeGroot-Nesdahl has served the South Dakota Synod of the Evangelical Lutheran Church in America as Bishop since 1995. She is the second woman (of only two) to be elected bishop in the ELCA. She previously served as an assistant to a bishop and as pastor in three parishes in metropolitan and small-town settings. She and her husband, Gary, are the parents of three teenagers and live in Sioux Falls. The whole family recently traveled to Africa where Andrea represented the ELCA at the World Council of Churches Assembly in Zimbabwe and visited South Dakota's companion synod in Cameroon.

25. Ann E. Helmke is founder and Animating Director of the peaceCENTER in San Antonio, Texas. Prior to this interfaith setting, she served Grace Lutheran, an inner-city church. Ann coordinated the San Antonio Gang Peace Summit in 1994, which aided in the largest and most continuous crime-rate decrease in the city's history. Ann received the San Antonio Peacemaker of the Year award in 1995. Her ministry faithfully is shared and supported by her two daughters (Rachel Lora [eighteen] and Kara Joy [twelve]) and her husband, Mark, an attorney and vice president of the Southeastern Texas Synod (ELCA).